Sarah

Sarah

The Life of Sarah Bernhardt

———— ✤ ————

ROBERT GOTTLIEB

Yale

UNIVERSITY

PRESS

NEW HAVEN AND LONDON

Frontispiece: Sarah in *Hernani*.

Designed and typeset by Gregg Chase in Janson.
Printed in the United States of America.

Library of Congress Cataloging-in-Publication Data

Gottlieb, Robert, 1931–
Sarah : the life of Sarah Bernhardt / Robert Gottlieb.
p. cm.—(Jewish Lives)
Includes bibliographical references and index.
ISBN 978-0-300-14127-6 (cloth : alk. paper) 1. Bernhardt, Sarah, 1844–1923.
2. Actresses—France—19th century—Biography. 3. Actresses—France—20th
century—Biography. I. Title.
PN2638.B5.G68 2010
792'.028092—dc22
[B]
2010001900

A catalogue record for this book is available from the British Library.

This paper meets the requirements of ANSI/NISO Z39.48-1992
(Permanence of Paper).

10 9 8 7 6 5 4 3 2 1

BOOKS BY ROBERT GOTTLIEB

Reading Dance
(editor)

Balanchine: The Ballet Master

Reading Lyrics
(edited with Robert Kimball)

Reading Jazz
(editor)

*The Everyman's Library
Collected Stories by Rudyard Kipling*
(editor)

The Journals of John Cheever
(editor)

*A Certain Style:
The Art of the Plastic Handbag, 1949–1959*

For my wife, Maria Tucci

CONTENTS

Sarah

The Life of Sarah Bernhardt

One summer day, some months before her death, my grandmother, who was then seventy-eight years old, summoned me to her room in the Manor House of Penhoët and said: "Lysiane, you are a writer and some day you must write a book about me. So I am going to entrust you with certain objects and certain documents."

"But," I replied, "you have already written your memoirs yourself."

"Yes, but they stop in 1881 and we are now in 1922. Besides," she added with a smile, "perhaps I did not tell everything."

—Lysiane Bernhardt

I

SARAH BERNHARDT was born in July or September or October of 1844. Or was it 1843? Or even 1841?

She was born in Paris at 5, rue de l'École de Médecine (that's where the plaque is). Or was it 32 (or 265), rue St. Honoré? Or 22, rue de la Michandière?

We'll never know, because the official records were destroyed when the Hôtel de Ville, where they were stored, went up in flames during the Commune uprising of 1871. With someone else that would hardly matter, because we'd have no reason to doubt whatever he or she told us. But dull accuracy wasn't Bernhardt's strong point: She was a complete realist when dealing with her life but a relentless fabulist when recounting it. Why settle for anything less than the best story? For the ultimate word on Sarah's veracity we can turn to Alexandre Dumas *fils*, who, referring to her famous thinness, remarked affection-ately, "You know, she's such a liar, she may even be fat!"

We do know who her mother was, but her father remains an enigma. We *think* we know who the father of her son was, but can we be sure? Everything about her early years is elu-sive—no letters, no reminiscences of family or friends, and what few documents that exist, highly obscure. Her singularly unreliable memoirs, *My Double Life*, carry her through her first thirty-five or so years, and they're the only direct testimony we have of her life until she's in her mid-teens. Yet despite her obfuscations, avoidances, lapses of memory, disingenuous rev-elations, and just plain lies, we can track her path, and (more important) begin to grasp her essential nature.

There are three basic components to her experience of childhood, two of them enough to derail an ordinary mortal: Her mother didn't love her, and she had no father. What she did have was her extraordinary will: to survive, to achieve, and—most of all—to have her own way. She would like us to believe that it was at the age of nine that she adopted her lifelong mot-to, *Quand même*. You can translate *quand même* in a number of (unsatisfactory) ways: "Even so." "All the same." "Despite everything." "Nevertheless." "Against all odds." "No matter what." They all fit both the child she was and the woman she was to become.

The mother—Judith, Julie, Youle Van Hard—had her own reserves of strength and willpower, but unlike Sarah's, they were hidden under layers of lazy charm and an almost phleg-matic disposition. She was a pretty blonde, she played and sang appealingly, she was a congenial hostess, and she welcomed the expensive attentions of a variety of men-about-town. As a result, she had managed to fashion for herself a comfortable niche in the higher reaches of the demimonde of the Paris of the 1840s. Never one of the great courtesans—*les grandes horizontales*—she nevertheless always had one or two well-to-do "protectors" to squire her around the elegant spas of Europe.

Youle conducted a relaxed salon to which a group of distinguished men gravitated, among them her lover Baron Larrey, who was the Emperor Louis-Napoléon's doctor (his father had been chief medical officer of the first Napoléon's armies); the composer Rossini; the novelist and playwright Dumas *père;* and the duc de Morny, known as the most powerful man in France, who was Louis-Napoléon's illegitimate half-brother. Morny was a highflying and successful financier as well as the president of the *Corps Legislatif,* exerting immense political influence without entering the field of politics himself. It was Rosine, Youle's younger, prettier, livelier sister, who was Morny's mistress—except when Youle herself was; in these circles, it hardly mattered. The important thing, since it would prove crucial to Sarah's life, was that Morny was a regular fixture in the intimate life of the family.

Youle and Rosine had come a long way. Their mother, Julie (or Jeanette) Van Hard—a Jewish girl either German or Dutch in origin—had married Maurice Bernard, a Jewish oculist in Amsterdam. There were five or six daughters (Sarah doesn't make it easy to keep track of her aunts) and at least one son, Édouard Bernard, who, like Sarah, eventually morphed into "Bernhardt." When their mother died and their father remarried, Youle and Rosine struck out on their own, first to Basel, then on to London and Le Havre, where in 1843 Youle—perhaps fifteen years old—gave birth to illegitimate twin girls, both of whom died within days. Documents about their birth provide the first verifiable data we have about her. Although the twins' father isn't named, the supposition is that he was a young naval officer named Morel, from a prominent Havrais family.

Undeterred, the ambitious Youle quickly set out for Paris, her daytime occupation seamstress, her nighttime career a quick ascent into the demimonde. Soon, two of her sisters followed her to Paris: the younger Rosine, who would surpass her in the ranks of courtesans, and the older Henriette, who made a solid marriage to a well-off businessman, Felix Faure.

(The Faures would be the only respectable bourgeoisie of Sarah's youth.) Quickly—or already?—Youle was pregnant again, with Sarah, whose name appears in various documents as Rosine Benardt (her application for the Conservatoire) and Sarah Marie Henriette Bernard (her certificate of baptism).

The most likely candidate for the honor of having fathered Sarah is that same naval Morel. His (or someone's) family lawyer in Havre later administered a sum of money that Sarah was to inherit on her marriage; he also at times involved himself in the child's future. Another suggested candidate was a brilliant young law student in Paris with whom Youle lived happily in poverty (a likely story!), until his family forced them apart. (It's *La Dame aux camélias*, Sarah's greatest success, before the fact.) Sarah never names her father in *My Double Life*, although on her certificate of baptism, filled out when she was thirteen, he's called Édouard Bernhardt. But isn't that the name of her mother's brother? Looking for consistency in Sarah's early history is a fruitless task.

What matters, finally, is that there *was* no father. In *My Double Life*, Sarah sketches a highly implausible tale. She rarely saw him—his business, whatever it was, kept him away from Paris until he suddenly died in Italy. He did, however, come with Youle to enroll Sarah in the aristocratic convent school he insisted she attend—apparently the only occasion on which the three of them did something together. As she tells it, on the night before she was to be installed in the school, her father said to her, "Listen to me, Sarah. If you are very good at the convent I will come in four years and fetch you away, and you shall travel with me and see some beautiful countries." "Oh, I will be good!" she exclaimed; "I'll be as good as Aunt Henriette." "This was my Aunt Faure," she writes. "Everybody smiled."

After dinner, she and her father had a serious talk. "He told me things that were sad which I had never heard before. Although I was so young I understood, and I was on his knee with my head resting on his shoulder. I listened to everything he said and cried silently, my childish mind distressed by his words. Poor Father! I was never, never to see him again." Nor are we to hear about him again except when Sarah remarks in passing that he was "handsome as a god" (what else could he have been? No parent of Sarah's could be merely good-looking), and that she "loved him for his seductive voice and his slow, gentle gestures."

It's clear that Sarah needed to believe that she was important to this shadowy father—that he was lovingly concerned about her even when he was absent. That impression is strengthened by the father (and mother) she invented for a ridiculous novel she wrote in her old age. In *Petite Idole* (*The Idol of Paris*), Espérance—the beautiful beloved daughter of a refined family—is destined to become a great actress at a far younger age than Sarah did, and with far less difficulty. Espérance is worshiped by her all-loving, all-understanding, and highly distinguished parents, who are prepared to sacrifice anything and everything (including the philosopher-father's induction into the Académie Française) to their daughter's well-being. (She ends up marrying a duke.) The pathetic act of wish-fulfillment that this fiction represents only serves to underline the deep traumas of Sarah's childhood. After more than half a century, the most illustrious woman of her time was still grappling with having been an unwanted and unloved child.

She narrated her story more than once—in her memoirs, of course, but also, toward the end of her life, both to her granddaughter Lysiane and to Lysiane's husband, the playwright Louis Verneuil. Each of them wrote a hagiographic biography of her based presumably on her account. (Verneuil was obsessed with Sarah, and he and Lysiane were divorced within months of Sarah's death, suggesting that their marriage was more about their grandmother than about each other.)

There was also a series of interviews that in 1898 Sarah gave to a friendly journalist, Jules Huret, from which, with her encouragement, he fashioned a biography.

And then there's a self-serving but sporadically convincing account of Sarah's birth by Thérèse Berton, whose late husband, Pierre, had been Sarah's leading man and leading lover for a number of years as her career was getting under way. Mme Berton is obviously filled with resentment and envy—with real rancor—toward Sarah, but she did spend years in her company, on the endless tours that Berton and Bernhardt conducted long after their affair had turned into collegiality. (He was a very good actor, and an excellent foil for her stardom.) Mme Berton assures us that Sarah confided in her totally, with the firm understanding that after Sarah died, Berton would tell the whole truth and nothing but. Otherwise, of course, she would never have set pen to paper.

"Have I the right to divulge this secret of all secrets, for nearly fourscore years locked in the breast of the greatest woman of four epochs? . . . Have I the right to tear the shroud from that dead face, and let the world gaze afresh on a long-familiar visage, only to find a new and wondrously changed entity beneath?" After an intense struggle, having "fought it out with myself through long, sleepless nights," Mme Berton decides that she *does* have the right—indeed, the obligation. "The last thing [Sarah] wanted was for the facts of her life to be at the mercy of imaginative chroniclers."

The Berton version: In Frankfurt, pretty young Julie Van Hard falls madly in love with a young French courier in the diplomatic corps and follows him to Paris, until his parents (of noble birth) step in, whereupon he abandons her without warning and without money. For weeks, "a stranger in a strange land," little Julie "lived as best she might. . . . Whatever she did, no one can blame her." (In other words, Sarah's mother sold herself.) Eventually she struck up an acquaintance with a law student, also from Le Havre and "one of the wildest youngsters in the Latin Quarter," who was registered on the books of the University of Paris as Édouard Bernhardt. However, the family name of this man, according to what Sarah learned later, was actually de Therard, and his baptismal name was Paul. It was he who rented the little flat on the rue de l'École de Médecine in which Sarah was—or wasn't—born. But two weeks before that was to happen, Édouard/Paul Bernhardt/de Therard returned to Le Havre, though "he wrote ardent letters to the forsaken mother and sent regular sums for the child's support."

Can any or all of this be true? It would make sense, if the father was studying at the University of Paris, that the flat was in the rue de l'École de Médecine, in the heart of the Latin Quarter. (A more likely because more matter-of-fact explanation is that this flat was where Julie's midwife lived.) Might it have been that with a baby coming, Therard took on a variation of Julie's name, Bernard, rather than use his own, and borrowed her brother's name as well? Again, we'll never know.

What motivated all of Sarah's lies and deceptions about her birth, Thérèse Berton would have us believe, was her anguish over her illegitimacy's being revealed to the world. Yet this seems highly unlikely, given that in her circles illegitimacy was hardly an impediment to social acceptance. After all, the duc de Morny himself was proudly illegitimate (his mother being Queen Hortense of Holland), and—more directly to the point—neither Sarah nor her son, Maurice, ever attempted to hide *his* illegitimacy. Indeed, Sarah flaunted this irregularity, perpetually joking about who Maurice's father might be.

Does it matter who Sarah's father actually was? Yes, because it mattered to her. *Family* mattered to her. She named her son Maurice after her grandfather; she herself was named after her Aunt Rosine; she was compulsively attentive to her mother and her two half-sisters as long as they lived; and Maurice was, from first to last, the most important person in her life. (One of her biographers explains that strong attachment to family is a well-known Jewish characteristic.) Her father, whoever he was, clearly did not share this characteristic, but then no one has ever suggested that *he* was Jewish.

However powerful a presence her absent father was in

Sarah and her mother (Youle)

Sarah's psyche, Youle's actual presence—when she bothered to be present—was just as powerful. One can sympathize with this teenage girl, groping for a foothold in the Paris demimonde, who found herself on her own, and with the additional impediment of a baby. Perhaps she resented the baby's existence. Perhaps she found it hard to be reminded of the absconded father. But for whatever reasons, from the start Youle was not very interested in her child. It wasn't lack of maternal feeling—when her second daughter, Jeanne (father unknown), was born, in 1851, Youle adored her, pampered her, and made it painfully obvious that she loved her far more than she did Sarah.

By the time Sarah was three, she had been sent away to a small village near Quimperle in Brittany to be cared for by a nurse who had probably performed the same services for Édouard Bernhardt when he himself was little—that's Édouard the presumed father, not Édouard the uncle. There, in a modest peasant dwelling, Sarah spent her early childhood, her first language Breton rather than French, and with no educa-

Sarah's sisters: Régine, left, and Jeanne

tion of any kind. "My mother's age was nineteen; I was three years old; my two aunts were seventeen and twenty years of age; another aunt was fifteen, and the eldest was twenty-eight, but the latter lived in Martinique and was the mother of six children. My grandmother was blind, my grandfather dead, and my father had been in China for the last two years. I have no idea why he had gone there." (Nor do we; nor is there any reason to believe that he *was* there.) Youle almost never came to see her. Sarah was essentially a foster child.

Then, still according to Sarah, there took place a frightening accident that led eventually to a new life. One day, with the nurse out in the field gathering potatoes and the good woman's husband laid up in bed, unable to move, the little girl managed to fall into the fireplace. Some neighbors heard her foster father's screams, and "I was thrown, all smoking, into a large pail of fresh milk." Within days, "My aunts came from all parts of the world, and my mother, in the greatest alarm, hastened from Brussels with Baron Larrey. . . . I have been

9

told since that nothing was more painful to witness and yet so charming as my mother's despair." At last Sarah had Youle's attention. "Mother, admirably beautiful, looked like a Madonna with her golden hair and her eyes fringed with such long lashes that they made a shadow on her cheeks when she lowered her eyes. She distributed money on all sides, she would have given her golden hair, her slender white fingers, her tiny feet, her life itself, in order to save her child." And she was as sincere in her despair and her love as in her usual forgetfulness. Sarah was slathered with a mask of butter that was changed every two hours. It worked! "I didn't even have a scar, it seems. My skin was rather too bright a pink, but that was all."

After some weeks, Sarah's story continues, Youle transported her, the nurse, and the nurse's husband to a little house at Neuilly, on the banks of the Seine, where they spent the next two years. Youle, traveling again, sent "money, bonbons, and toys" and, according to Thérèse Berton, saw Sarah only once during that time—and that once only by accident.

Louis Verneuil, however, in his biography based on what Sarah told him at the end of her life, makes no mention of falling into fires and dousings in milk pails and slatherings of butter but simply states that since travel to Brittany was long and arduous and wasted a lot of Youle's time whenever "the whim seized her to kiss her child," she installed Sarah and her nurse in Neuilly "in order to be less inconvenienced." This, given what we know of Youle, sounds entirely plausible.

Then, an event straight out of *Les Misérables*. The foster father dies, and the nurse remarries and moves with her new husband, a concierge, into an apartment house on the rue de Provence in the fashionable "boulevard" section of Paris. She doesn't know where Youle is. She has lost Aunt Rosine's address. Sarah has simply been misplaced and more or less forgotten. Moreover, the tiny space above the courtyard where the concierge lives is dark and cramped and gloomy: There's only a single small window, and Sarah longs for the open sky and the greenery she knows and loves from Brittany and Neuilly. "I want to go away. . . . It's all black, black! It's ugly! I want to see the ceiling of the street!" And one day a miracle happens! A carriage enters the courtyard and an elegant lady inquires about an apartment in the building. Yes—it's Aunt Rosine! Sarah flings her scruffy self onto this exquisite person, and Rosine, startled to come upon her niece in these circumstances and giving some money to the nurse, promises to return the next day to fetch her. (Youle, of course, is away traveling.)

But Sarah has no reason to believe that Tante Rosine will keep her promise, and is so distraught that she flings herself in front of her aunt's carriage as she's leaving. "After that I knew nothing more; everything seemed dark. . . . I had broken my arm in two places and injured my left kneecap. I only came to myself again a few hours later, to find that I was in a beautiful wide bed which smelled very nice." Soon Youle rushes to her side, as do the aunts and cousins, and Sarah spends the next two years recovering, with only vague memories of being petted and in "a chronic state of torpor."

So goes the more dramatic than credible story as told in Sarah's memoirs and obediently repeated by most of her biographers. It's improved upon by Thérèse Berton, who has Sarah not merely falling in front of Rosine's carriage but dashing herself to the courtyard pavement from the little window. On the other hand, Sarah told Jules Huret that it was her mother, not Rosine, who turned up on that traumatic day in the rue de Provence, and "I fell out of the window in my haste to reach her!" Cooler heads prefer the theory that Youle was already living in the rue de Provence (as she was several years later, according to the official documents concerning Jeanne's birth) and that it was she herself who had installed the nurse and her husband in the concierge's lodge.

Dramatic scenes were always Sarah's forte, and fires, defenestrations, and abandonment were more interesting to her— and no doubt less painful—than the obvious truth that Youle was a slapdash and irresponsible mother. But the heightened fictions Sarah indulged in also masked an intense emotional reality. As Ruth Brandon, one of her most perceptive biographers, put it, "Certainly it seemed likely that the central proposition of Sarah's account is true—that, physically or metaphorically, she felt her mother was lost to her and that, physically or metaphorically, she had to jump from a window and break her bones in order to gain her attention."

II

BY THE TIME Sarah had recovered from whatever physical problems she may have had (apart from her broken bones, she had an inherited predisposition to tuberculosis), it finally occurred to her mother that she was completely untutored. At the age of seven she couldn't read, write, or do the simplest arithmetic. The answer was school (also the answer to getting Sarah out of Youle's way, particularly since she was now pregnant with Jeanne). And so it was decided that Sarah would be sent to Mme Fressard's fashionable boarding school in the suburb of Auteuil—out of sight but within easy reach.

She remained there for two years, indeed learning to read and write and even making a stab at arithmetic—and also, she tells us, learning to sing rounds and embroider handkerchiefs (for her absent mother, of course; Youle almost never came to see her). For the first time in her life there were friends; Mme Fressard was kind; there was a big garden; there was a young actress from the Comédie-Française who came weekly to recite poetry to the girls. Sarah was entranced by her, and at night would sit on her bed reciting from Racine's great religious drama *Athalie:* "*Tremble, fille digne de moi.*" (In her seventies, she would finally play Athalie.) When the other girls laughed at her, she tells us, "I would rush about to the right and the left, kicking and hitting them." There were many such fits of temper, and they would leave her in the sickroom for two or three days afterward. They were like attacks of madness, she said.

It was also at Auteuil, according to Thérèse Berton, that Sarah was appearing in a little school play (as the Queen of the Fairies) when her mother, Aunt Rosine, and the duc de Morny turned up in the middle of the second scene, reducing Sarah to paralyzing stage fright. She collapsed in tears and ran to her room, to which her mother followed her and, looking at her coldly, said, "And to think that this is a child of mine!" It was Morny who comforted her: "Never mind, *ma petite*. You'll show them all how to act one of these days, won't you?" (This latter remark is so obviously an invention that one wonders whether the whole incident isn't an invention, too.) Having sobbed herself into yet another fever and four days in bed, Sarah kept thinking, "Why had my mother been so cruel, so cold to her daughter? I knew that another child had been born the year before [apparently Sarah had not yet encountered her sister Jeanne], and with a child's intuition I hit upon the right answer. Mother loved the baby more than she loved me—if, indeed, she loved me at all."

Sarah went on to confide to Berton, "Alas! this was not the last time that my mother's chilly behavior toward me threw me into a paroxysm of misery resulting in illness. I never grew callous to her disapproval of me; her cutting criticisms always had the power to wound me to the heart." (In fact, Youle never really liked or praised her daughter's acting, even after she had been acclaimed France's greatest actress.) How much of this story of Sarah's, or Berton's version of it, actually took place is open to question, but not the intensity of Sarah's love and longing for her distant and disapproving mother.

According to Berton, Youle came to visit Sarah only three times during her two years at Auteuil, and her father only once. One day she was summoned from her studies to Mme Fressard's office to find there "a very well-dressed man of about thirty, with a waxed moustache." After talking with her for ten minutes or so ("Why, she is growing into quite a little beauty!"), he went away, leaving Fressard to remark, "I should think you would love your father very, very much. He is such a handsome man." "How can I love him?" she replied. "I have never seen him before."

This is not, however, what Sarah told Louis Verneuil. "Édouard Bernhardt" came at least several times to Auteuil and, although he was satisfied with the school at first, he eventually concluded that her education there was not what it should be—in particular, her religious education. Since, Sarah explained, it was her father who paid the school bills, it was he who made the decisions about her education. (Youle paid for her clothes.) And what he decided was that Sarah would now be sent to the equally fashionable Grandchamps convent school in Versailles. Whereas the Jewish Youle would hardly be eager to see her daughter raised a Catholic, there were reasons why such a move made sense. If Sarah were to enter a more respectable world than her courtesan mother inhabited, she had to learn how to speak, move, behave like a lady, things she was unlikely to learn in her mother's all too louche—and predominantly male—orbit.

One day when she was nine, apparently without warning, Sarah was informed that on her father's orders she was being removed from Mme Fressard's and taken to the convent. This precipitated another violent burst of fury. "The idea that I was to be ordered about without any regard to my own wishes or inclinations put me into an indescribable rage." She rolled on the floor, screamed, ran into the garden, and threw herself into the pond before, exhausted, she was subdued and taken away in Aunt Rosine's carriage. "I stayed three days in her house, as I was so feverish that my life was said to be in danger."

Rest was prescribed, and for several weeks Sarah stayed in the Faures' country house, playing with her cousins, fishing in the stream. It was then that, dared by one of the cousins to jump over a wide ditch, she fell, broke her wrist, and "while I was being carried away, exclaimed furiously: 'Yes, I would do it again, *quand même*, if anyone dared me again. And all my life I will always do what I want to.'" This is the moment, she would have us believe, that she chose *Quand même* as her motto. (Others report that it was years later.) Her Aunt Henriette, whom she disliked, was not amused by her ragamuffin behavior, but as always her uncle Faure was kind and understanding. She was to respect his opinions and think fondly of him all her life, perhaps amused by his having escaped his marriage by becoming a Carthusian monk.

Youle, with perhaps more feeling for her daughter than Sarah was ever able to acknowledge, returned from her own sickbed abroad so that she herself could take Sarah to Versailles. They arrived at the convent door, Sarah in terror because the building looked like a prison. And then the door in the grating opened, and she fell in love with the round little woman who welcomed her. "I saw the sweetest and merriest face imaginable. . . . She looked so kind, so energetic, and so gay that I flung myself into her arms. It was Mother Ste. Sophie, the superior of the Grandchamps Convent." Quickly, the reverend mother soothed her by telling her that she could have a little garden of her own. "The convent no longer seemed to me like a prison but like Paradise."

Sarah would spend six years under the benign influence of Mother Ste. Sophie, who clearly understood her, loved her, and nurtured her. She had grasped at once that Sarah was a child who could not be coerced—who would always defy authority. But she also grasped that Sarah had a loving heart, and would respond eagerly to affection and sympathy. According to Lysiane, Youle said to Mother Ste. Sophie, "You have mastered my little wild animal." "Oh, no!" the superior responded. "I have merely tamed her."

From the first, the child was tempestuous—a scamp and a ringleader, and certainly not an exemplary student: Her only good subjects were geography and art. Her greatest passion was for animals—she collected crickets, lizards, spiders (to which she gleefully fed flies). She was always in trouble, and three times on the verge of being expelled for some outrageous prank. But the other girls looked up to her: "In short, I became a personality, and that was enough for my childish pride." Even so, Sarah tells us, she overheard Mother Ste. Sophie whisper to someone, "This child is one of the best we have here. She will be perfect once she has received the Chrism"—that is, been baptized.

She also had her first stage success, playing the Angel Raphael in a little dramatization of the Apocryphal story of Tobias curing his father's blindness. She was desperate to be chosen for a part, desolate when she wasn't, and ecstatic when the little girl who had been cast was so overcome with fear that she couldn't go on. Needless to say, in Sarah's account of this event she triumphed. The occasion for the performance was a visit to the convent by the archbishop of Paris, who promised to return for the little Jewish girl's baptism. (Alas, before that could happen, he was murdered by a demented priest whom he had excommunicated.)

The subject of her conversion to Catholicism was a crucial one, and on May 21, 1856, mostly at the insistence of her father, Sarah—soon to be twelve years old—was baptized; a week later she took her first communion. The ever-practical Youle had arranged for Jeanne (now aged five) and the latest addition to the family, Régine (aged two), to be baptized along with their older sister. As we have seen, Sarah's certificate of baptism names Édouard Bernhardt as her father, and he had promised to be there for the occasion but had died unexpectedly a few weeks earlier in Pisa. That tragedy, combined with Sarah's indulging in a fervid (or morbid?) outburst of religiosity, led to one of her typical collapses, followed by pneumonia—fever, total exhaustion, "fears for her life." It was agreed that she needed a long rest, and Youle took the family off to a fashionable resort in the Pyrenees, where Sarah recovered her health and high spirits and began to acquire a menagerie, starting with a train of goats she planned to take back to the convent. ("I asked Mama quite seriously whether I might become a goatherd.") After the usual dramas, two goats were allowed (for their milk), plus one blackbird.

The years at the convent accomplished what they had been meant to accomplish. "The little Jewish girl" had learned the manners and speech of upper-class Paris, and now not only was officially a Catholic but had thrown herself, with her typical dramatic intensity, into her new religion with the idea of becoming a nun (since she couldn't be a goatherd). Her passionate desire to stay on permanently in the convent was something not to be considered by Youle, nor—unsurprisingly—did Mother Ste. Sophie detect much of a true calling in the unruly Sarah. And then yet another prank, followed by yet another attack of pneumonia. ("I was twenty-three days between life and death. . . . Mother Ste. Sophie never left me for an instant.") This time when Youle collected her and took her back to Paris it was for the last time: Sarah's convent days were over, although she was still determined to become a teaching sister. That was not to happen, but she assures us that her memories of her beloved mother superior remained a lifelong inspiration to her.

III

IT WAS 1859, and Sarah was almost fifteen*—more or less a grown woman. The big question was what to do with her. There weren't many choices. The convent was now out of the question. A marriage into society was not really in the cards—despite her respectable education, she was the illegitimate daughter of a Jewish courtesan. Yet was she cut out to live the demimonde existence of her mother and her Aunt Rosine? It didn't seem so— her looks were striking but unconventional, her behavior more so. And she wasn't interested. A marriage into the bourgeoisie?

*If we accept 1844 as her birth year, and it's as good a guess as any.

Sarah's Aunt Rosine

That was Youle's preference, and the sooner the better—fifteen was the legal age for getting married, and Sarah's marriage would spare her mother further expense as well as distancing her sullen, sickly presence from Youle's ultraworldly life.

For the moment, Youle temporized, hiring a well-born, pious, and affectionate lady—Mlle de Brabender—to serve as Sarah's governess and chaperone. (Her great recommendation: She had been the tutor of a grand duchess in the Imperial Court of Russia.) Luckily, Sarah loved her, and was loved in return.

Even more luckily, upstairs from the grand apartment which Youle and Rosine now shared lived a young married (soon to be widowed) woman named Mme Guérard (her husband was an elderly medievalist scholar) who had become a gentle, cheerful presence in Youle's life—they gossiped, they played cards, they exchanged confidences. From the moment she and Sarah met, they were drawn together in what would prove to be the strongest friendship of Sarah's life—for more than forty years Guérard (Sarah always called her *mon p'tit dame*) would be

Sarah and Mme Guérard   The duc de Morny

at Sarah's side as her most loyal supporter. "She saw me come
into the world," Sarah told Huret—certainly untrue—"and she
was present at the birth of my son, Maurice, and of my granddaughter." And she was totally trusted. (When, for instance, on
Sarah's first American tour, she insisted upon being paid in gold
coins before every performance, it was Guérard who carried the
haul around in a leather bag.) Sarah was to say that Mme Guérard's death, in 1900, was the worst blow she ever suffered, and
you can understand why. Not only was she eternally supportive
and unjudgmental, but she was witness to Sarah's life well into
her fifties. When Guérard died, Sarah's youth, her struggles to
achieve success, her greatest triumphs, her affairs of the heart,
went with her. She was the good mother Sarah had never had.
Yet she was so discreet we don't even know her first name.

        Mme Guérard was present at one of the most dramatic
scenes of Sarah's youth, repeated in every account, beginning
with her own. She's sulking around the house with nothing to
do when Maman tells her to put on her blue frock and come

to the drawing room: There's to be a family council to decide her future. When she arrives, there on stage are all the major players in her life: her mother and Aunt Rosine, of course; her Aunt and Uncle Faure; Mlle de Brabender; Mme Guérard; her godfather, M. Régis; an old friend of the family's, M. Meydieu; from Le Havre, Maître G, the notary of her father's family ("my father's evil genius"); and—the star of the scene—the duc de Morny, in his capacity of lover and adviser to the sisters, looking on in his amused, reserved way.

The curtain goes up. Sarah is still insisting on the convent. "You have to be rich to enter a convent," says the evil Maître G, "and you haven't got a sou." Sarah whispers, "I have the money that Papa left me." Maître G: "Your father left some money to get you married." Sarah: "Well, then, I'll marry the Bon Dieu." Youle interjects that that would make her very unhappy: "You know that after your sister, I love you better than anyone in the world."

Finally, the duc de Morny grows bored (who can blame him?) and rises to go. "Do you know what you ought to do with this child? Send her to the Conservatoire." "The Conservatoire?" thinks Sarah. "What was that? What did it mean?" How could she, practically a nun, dream of appearing on the stage?

The other players disappear, and Sarah is startled yet again when told she's being taken to the theater that very night—to the Comédie-Française itself! She's never been to a real play. She and Youle and M. Régis and Mlle de Brabender proceed by carriage to the theater and take their seats in a box belonging to that habitué of Youle's salon, Dumas *père*. "When the curtain slowly rose, I thought I was going to faint. It was as if the curtain of my future life was being raised. Those columns—Racine's *Britannicus* was being played—were to be my palaces, the friezes above were to be my skies, and those boards were to bend under my frail weight." During the second play, Molière's *Amphitryon*, she bursts into sobs, to the amusement of the audience. Her godfather explodes. "What a little idiot the child is!"

"This," remarks Sarah, neatly rounding off a chapter of her memoirs, "was the debut of my artistic life."

However, she's disgraced herself and seriously irritated her mother by her wayward behavior. Dumas himself escorts them home from the theater, helps carry her to her room (she's fallen asleep from excitement and emotional exhaustion), and bending over her, gives her a kiss and whispers, "Good night, little star." This last far-fetched flourish comes from Lysiane's account. Sarah explains to her granddaughter why she left the Dumas episode out of her memoirs: "Well, before he died, he had a bitter quarrel with my family and I promised Maman I would never talk about all that. But now! It's so long ago now! More than half a century."

As for the accuracy of the entire episode, it's highly suspect, beginning with the idea that she had never seen a play. Youle was living at this time in the neighborhood of the Français, and others note that Sarah used to hang around the theater, chatting with the actors and actresses who would sneak her into performances.

Besides, a family council of these proportions to ponder the fate of a troublesome adolescent? The only thing that seems genuine about the story is Sarah's lifelong need to create scenes of which she was the center of attention—the more supporting actors, the better. A far more believable scenario comes from Louis Verneuil, the confidant to whom Sarah seems to have spoken with the least concealment or embroidery. At seventy-eight, what did she have to lose by telling the simple truth? First, she reveals that Youle was the long-running and final mistress of Morny, who took an interest in her welfare and that of her children. Having observed how much the problem of Sarah was exasperating Youle, he determined to help free her of this nagging worry. Verneuil: "One evening when, by some miracle, the only other guest was Mme Guérard, the duc de Morny said carelessly: 'If my name were Sarah, I know very well what I would do.' The little girl, as usual, was lost in reverie. She started up, 'Well, what would you do?' 'I would try to enter the Conservatoire.'"

At first Sarah balked, but the prospect of hard work toward a definable goal attracted her—no one ever accused her of being lazy!—and the next day she "searched in her schoolbooks for the tragedies of Racine and Corneille, and immediately began to learn all the parts, male and female without distinction." Verneuil sums it up neatly: "At the age of almost sixteen years she had never thought of acting. In order to take her off her mother's hands who did not like her, one of the latter's lovers said one fine day: 'Why not try and make an actress of her?' In order to get away from her mother, whose life as a kept woman shocked her, Sarah replied: 'All right, let's try.'"

Then follows the last of the endlessly regurgitated dramatic episodes of Sarah's youth. After a month of feverish preparation—coached by Dumas himself, among others—Sarah, attended by Mlle de Brabender and Mme Guérard, turns up at the Conservatoire for her audition. Surrounding her are self-assured boys and girls, all of them accompanied by family, who poke fun at her dowdy escorts. When her moment comes, the bored functionary who's ushering her inside to the judges asks her what play she'll be acting. "*L'École des femmes*," she replies. And who will be cueing her? But no one had mentioned that she would need a partner, and it was now too late to find one. In that case, she says, she won't act a scene from a play but instead will recite the famous la Fontaine fable *Les Deux Pigeons*. Unheard of! "Is this a joke? This isn't a nursery school!" one of the examiners exclaims. But Sarah persists.

Starting off, she falters, and the judges are irritated. But the benign head of the conservatory, Daniel Auber, the composer of such great successes as *Le Domino noir* and *Fra Diavolo*, encourages her to begin again, and within moments the entire group is mesmerized by her exquisite voice and perfect enunciation. On her way out, Auber asks her, "Is your name Sarah?" "Yes, sir." "Are you a Jewess?" "By birth, sir, but I have been baptized." "She's been baptized," Auber tells the jury, "and it would have been a pity for such a pretty child not to be." He also tells her not only that she's been accepted, but that two of the judges are vying to take her on as a student. Bursting with pride and excitement, she rushes to where her guardians and the other applicants are gathered and spreads the news. More commotion! No one is ever accepted on the instant; everyone else must wait for official notice. She's triumphed against the odds. Despite everything. *Quand même.*

No doubt Sarah charmed the examiners with her voice and her odd presence—so pale, so thin—but there was never a possibility of her being rejected by the Conservatoire. As Verneuil explains, during the audition "Auber quickly scribbled some words on a sheet of paper" and circulated it among his colleagues. "When they read the name of the duc de Morny, who was not only all-powerful but extremely well liked at the Français, they immediately became attentive and well disposed. . . . An hour later she was told that out of the hundred or two hundred candidates who had presented themselves, she was among the fifteen or twenty who had been admitted." Not only was she a protégée of Morny's—in fact, the daughter of his mistress—but the great man had condescended to call on his friend Auber in his office and explain what was what. No one in France would have considered offending the emperor's brother by ignoring such a recommendation. From the moment Morny came up with the idea of Sarah's becoming an actress, her acceptance by the Conservatoire was a certainty.

IV

SARAH WAS a dedicated—some say obsessive—student, even if she didn't agree with everything she was being taught. Decades later, she told her own students that, for instance, she had been instructed never to speak with her back to the audience—a lesson she deplored and ignored. Indeed, she was famous for the drama she could wring out of speeches delivered while turned upstage. She particularly loathed the strict lessons in stage deportment that insisted she had to memorize the specific ways a certain kind of character must automatically sit, stand, move.* The only way Sarah ever believed in was *her* way. Even so, she worked hard to correct what she agreed were real deficiencies, telling Jules Huret, "I had considerable difficulties to overcome. I inherited from my mother a serious defect in pronunciation—speaking with clenched teeth. In all the imitations of my style this point is seized upon. . . . To cure me of the habit, the Conservatoire teachers gave me little rubber balls, which prevented me from closing my mouth."

There are reports that she wasn't much liked by her fellow students—she was too unruly, too self-promoting. Yet she had friends, and the closest she'd come to a boyfriend. He was a student about her age named Paul Parfouru, who would later change his name to Paul Porel, become first a successful actor, then director of the Variétés theater and the Odéon, and the husband of France's great popular actress Réjane, the only rival Sarah really admired.

Long after Porel's death, his son, Jacques, wrote in his memoirs about a photograph of herself that Sarah had given his father. "Its tender inscription certainly leads one to think

---

* Corroboration of her memory of these act-by-numbers methods turns up in a letter from Charles Dickens to John Forster in 1856, only a few years before Sarah entered the Conservatoire: "There is a dreary classicality at [the Comédie-Française] calculated to freeze the marrow. . . . One tires of seeing a man, through any number of acts, remembering everything by patting his forehead with the flat of his hand, jerking out sentences by shaking himself, and piling them up in pyramids over his head with his right forefinger. And they have a generic small comedy-piece, where you see two sofas and three little tables, to which a man enters with his hat on, to talk to another man— and in respect of which you know exactly when he will get up from one sofa to sit on the other, and take his hat off one table to put it on the other—which strikes one quite as ludicrously as a good farce."

that there was more than a simple friendship between them." And Jacques was more forthcoming with biographers Arthur Gold and Robert Fizdale when they were researching *The Divine Sarah:* "Imagine, Jacques," his father had said to him, "you who worshipped Sarah, imagine what that fascinating woman was at sixteen—her verve, her incandescent smile, her energy!" Sarah and Paul Porel were to remain friends all their lives.

As always with Sarah, the children of her great friends adored her, and she them. (This was true not only of Jacques Porel but of Edmond Rostand's son—named Maurice after Maurice Bernhardt—who wrote an adoring book about her, and Lucien Guitry's son, the famous Sacha.) Jacques Porel's superb memoirs—alas, never translated into English—evoke her largeness of spirit, her warmth, her common sense, her generosity.

And from the unpublished memoirs of the senior Porel, from which Jacques quotes at length, we get perhaps as close as we'll ever get to a sense of Sarah at the Conservatoire. To begin with, Jacques mentions in passing that his father and Sarah were born in the same year: 1843. (So much for 1844.) They both graduated in July 1862, both of them having studied with Régnier and Provost, two great actors and magnificent pedagogues. "Even though he recognized her distinction, her originality, her grace, Provost didn't like her. Turbulent, always late, she both intrigued and maddened him; he was very hard on her." Coaching her in a scene from Voltaire's *Zaïre*, he kept her standing on a platform for two hours, "correcting every dubious gesture, every forced cry, every incorrect inflection. He was pitiless—and extremely interesting." And when it was over, he glared at her and handed down his verdict: "Well, there's a role you have to remember never to play." A dozen years later, she was to triumph in it: Provost may have been disagreeable to her, but she had learned everything he had to teach her. No momentary discomfort was going to stand between her and her new goal: to become the greatest actress in the world.

Her career at the Conservatoire, however, was hardly a

triumph. At the end of each of the two years of the curriculum, the students performed both a tragedy and a comedy scene before a jury. In 1861 she managed a second prize for tragedy and honorable mention for comedy, which somewhat encouraged her. In her second year she won nothing at all for tragedy— she had been certain she'd win first prize—and only the second prize for comedy. There were extenuating circumstances—a disaster with her hair, badly chosen roles forced on her—but although she had received good reports through the year, she was not only a disappointment in her own eyes but a failure and disgrace in her mother's, as Youle made clear when Sarah got home from the competition. Her godfather, M. Régis, Sarah reports in her memoirs, said to her, "Well, you were a failure. Why persist in going in for the theater? You're thin and you're small. Your face isn't bad close to, but at a distance it's ugly. And your voice doesn't carry." No wonder she was in despair when she went to bed that night. "Had there been any poison at hand I would have taken it," she told Thérèse Berton.

And then, at midnight, a note was slipped under her door by Mme Guérard: "While you were sleeping, the duc de Morny sent word to your mother telling her that your engagement at the Comédie-Française is confirmed. So, my darling, there's nothing to worry about—your future is secure." Morny had been to see Camille Doucet, overseer of the two official theaters—the Français and the Odéon—who was also a friend of the family's. The next day the formal letter of acceptance arrived, and the day after that Sarah presented herself at the theater ludicrously overdressed in what she described as "a hideous cabbage-green dress in which I looked like a monkey"—borrowed from Aunt Rosine at Youle's insistence—to receive her contract, which Youle had to sign: Sarah was still a minor. She was to earn only fifty francs a month, the beginner's salary, but she was a member of the Comédie-Française.

V

WHAT WAS she like at this critical juncture? What was her life? How did she appear to others?

Her most prominent characteristic was her thinness—it was her defining feature, derided and caricaturized everywhere for at least a quarter of a century. ("She's so thin that when she swallows a pill, she looks pregnant"; "When she takes a bath, the level of the water goes down.") To our eyes she doesn't look particularly thin in the countless representations of her that exist, but this was an age of well-developed women. Only after she had a serious abdominal operation in her middle age did people stop insisting on Bernhardt's thinness, harping instead on her youthfulness.

Fortunately for posterity, a series of astoundingly beautiful portraits of the young Sarah was taken by the great photographer Félix Nadar. (She may have been sixteen, or perhaps a year or two older.) She's posed calmly, meditatively, with a mantle of cloth draped carelessly around her shoulders. Her untamed hair bursts out around her face, looking darker than the red-gold that was its natural color. The eyes are startling and enigmatic—a number of observers noted that, depending on her mood, they changed color, from gray to green to blue. The forehead is high, the nose just slightly irregular (Jewish, they said). The effect is mysterious, intense, yet withheld; closer to tragic than assertive. She looks like no one else in the world.

Almost as famous as the Nadar portraits is an anonymous photograph of her, bare to the navel, a fan coquettishly held up to her face, one eye peeking out. Her breasts are small, piquant; her waist hardly tiny by today's standards. We can assume that she was paid to pose for this picture at a time, in the early 1860s, when she was desperately in need of money. But posing for photographers was completely natural to her—it was one of her lifelong avocations. (Several commentators have questioned whether Sarah was indeed the model for this ravishing image.)

The famous Nadar portraits

Her voice was considered *d'argent*—silvery—and rather weak; it would be years before she became known for her Voice of Gold. Her diction was exquisite—poetry was a natural language for her. She was short—not much above five feet tall. She was moderate in her eating and drinking. Her health was precarious, as it had been throughout her childhood, yet she was fun-loving and spontaneous—often too spontaneous for her own good. There's a vivid and affectionate description of her at work written in 1874 by the playwright Octave Feuillet, whose

play *Le Sphinx* featured Sarah as the second *jeune première* and her great pal and rival, the cheerful, pretty Sophie Croizette, as the lead. Writing to his wife, Feuillet reports:

> Unlike the other actresses, she turns up at rehearsals dressed to kill . . . velvet from head to foot. . . . With her hair all frizzy and usually holding onto a bunch of flowers, she rehearses seriously, the way she's supposed to, sometimes striking beautiful poses, à la Rachel. Then

when the scene's over, she bursts into dance, jumps
around, sits down at the piano to accompany herself in
a bizarre Negro song, which she sings very prettily. Then
she stands up and marches around like a circus clown,
munching on chocolates she carries in her bag and
fixing her lipstick. There's nothing more charming than
watching Sarah and Croizette, their mothers in tow
[in Sarah's case, of course, Mme Guérard], exiting the
theater together like two startled goddesses, noses up in
the air, their straw hats perched on top of their huge
blond hair-dos, twirling their parasols, chattering and
laughing at the top of their voices, heading for Chibouste's
patisserie where they'll stuff themselves with cake.

Clowning, singing, posing—all this no doubt reflected
her high spirits, but it also reflected her unquenchable need to
be the center of attention, off stage as well as on.

When she was starting out—at the Conservatoire, in her
early days at the Français—she was living at home, and still
under pressure from Youle to earn her keep. Even after she was
set on the path of the theater, the family kept doing its best to
marry her off—as she told Huret, to a glover, a tanner, and a
pharmacist. "My mother isn't married herself, yet she wants me
to be a wife! My mother is a Jewess, and she doesn't want her
daughter to be a nun!" she burst out one evening, according to
Thérèse Berton. (Can you wonder that Youle found her so exasperating?) Sarah, however, was determined to marry only for
love. At this point she rarely saw her mother, taking her meals
with Mlle de Brabender and little Régine in the nursery. She
was completely concentrated on her studies, even giving up her
art lessons, with which she had had considerable success, winning a prize given by her art school for a painting called *Winter
in the Champs-Élysées* and her first review—from the *Mercure de
France*, October 1860: "Mlle Bernhardt exhibits an extraordinary talent for one so young." (She was sixteen.)

A grimmer picture of her life at this time is to be found

Taken in Nadar's atelier

in the notorious roman à clef *The Life and Memoirs of Sarah Barnum* by her intimate-friend-turned-mortal-enemy Marie Colombier, a key figure in Sarah's life. They were close at the Conservatoire and after, and Colombier is an indispensable witness to Sarah's later youth—at home in Youle's apartment, and not only a colleague of Sarah's but a recipient of her confidences. Marie was a jolly, plump, sluttish girl, but also a sharp observer and a skilled and caustic writer. Her first book about Sarah, a narrative of the first Bernhardt tour of America, in 1880, was mordant but restrained. Her second, in which "Bernhardt" is turned into "Barnum"—a sly slap at Sarah's endless self-promotion—was written after the two women had had a furious falling-out, and it's vicious, slanderous, cruel, and virulently anti-Semitic. It's also clearly based, to a certain degree, on the truth. The problem for all of Sarah's biographers has been to distinguish between the truth and the slander.

In *Sarah Barnum*, Colombier harps on Youle's coldness toward her oldest daughter as well as on her avarice. M. Régis (her godfather, disguised as "M. Riges") is a guest at dinner.

> The Jewess [Youle] kept nudging Sarah's elbow. Having for a long while pretended not to take the hint, the young girl at last, influenced by a kick under the table, backed by a no less persuasive glance, was obliged to leave her seat and kiss their "good friend." Instantly the old man's eye glowed like a live coal played upon by a jet of oxygen. The young actress, absolutely transfixed by the maternal glares that never for an instant left her, suffered herself to be caressed while concealing her disgust, though she was powerless to subdue the shudder that passed over her each time the cold lips of M. Riges touched her throat or glued themselves to her delicate chin. Her docility was rewarded by the gift of a banknote. . . . Then the countenance of Mme Barnum lighted up. However, emboldened by his generosity, the old fellow drew Sarah down upon his knee. His left hand he cast about her waist, while with the other he smoothed her dress with a slow, agreeable caress . . .

The moment the old man departed, "her mother sat down at the table and took her banknote from her," and then, together with Aunt Rosette (Rosine), "reproached her with undisguised cruelty at having missed a chance with M. Riges, who would have given her two banknotes instead of one if she had only taken the trouble to make herself more fascinating." From now on, her mother raged, Sarah would have to make her own way in the world.

Also present at this repulsive scene were Sarah's two young sisters—and, are we to assume, Colombier herself? Certainly she intended her readers to take her story as barely disguised reportage.

If this were the only recorded document of Youle's determination to turn Sarah into a paying proposition—and how far is that, at bottom, from the story of Colette's Gigi?—we might put it down to Colombier's malice. But many people in Paris spoke openly of Youle's attempts to sell her daughters to her own former lovers, a fact confirmed by a famous reference in the gossipy Goncourt journals: "Overheard in Brebant's restaurant: 'The Sarah Bernhardt family—now, *there's* a family! The mother made whores of her daughters as soon as they turned thirteen.'" That could hardly have been the case with Sarah, who at thirteen was safely ensconced in her convent school, but the histories of Jeanne and Régine are considerably shadier.

It was during this period that Sarah collected her first real lover, a handsome thirty-ish hussar-about-town named Émile, le comte de Keratry. As usual, there are conflicting accounts of how they met. Sarah barely mentions him in her memoirs: Her aunt gives a dinner party to celebrate Sarah's engagement at the Comédie-Française (this is in 1862), at which are present Morny, Camille Doucet, Rossini (who, hearing her recite a poem, sat down at the piano and "improvised the most delightful harmony, which filled me with emotion"). And, oh yes: "The comte de Keratry was also present, an elegant young Hussar, who paid me some great compliments and invited me to go and recite some poetry at his mother's house." Could anything be more correct? She doesn't mention him again until they encounter each other, dramatically, during the siege of Paris almost a decade later.

Marie Colombier tells a different story. Maman and Aunt Rosine take Sarah to the theater with instructions to attract the right kind of man. It works! A handsome and chic young aristocrat follows her home. Soon they're a couple. Émile de Keratry, "as a jaded man about town, was intrigued by Sarah's bizarre mixture of naïveté and corruption. As for Sarah, though she was very attracted, she certainly didn't love him, and after his passionate embraces, she liked him even less. . . . Here she was already the consummate actress. She made her young officer feel he must persuade her to allow him to give her money and to be useful in other ways. When she got home, she threw the money on the table and said to her mother, 'I hope you won't bother me anymore.'" The next day, Youle rented a larger apartment with a separate entrance for Sarah. Her amorous career was launched.

VI

As for the launching of her stage career, for once the testimony is not conflicting. It was inauspicious, as even Sarah acknowledged in her memoirs. The first of the three traditional debuts for new actors took place on August 11, 1862, with Sarah in the title role of Racine's *Iphigénie*. She was in the grip of the stage fright—*le trac*—from which she was to suffer all her life. The audience was mostly made up of vacationing schoolteachers and out-of-towners. "I got through the play, but made no impression in my part."

Critical reaction was cool. France's most powerful theater critic, Francisque Sarcey, had this to say: "Mlle Bernhardt . . . is a tall,* pretty girl with a slender figure and a very pleasing expression, and the upper part of her face is remarkably beauti-

---

*This is the only reference to Sarah as tall that I know. Everyone else, from her godfather to the chef on one of her American tours, calls her small. The likely explanation for this discrepancy lies in the fact that both actresses and dancers generally look taller on stage than off—when you look at the clothes of stars like Marlene Dietrich and Joan Crawford you see that they were tiny. Sarah's co-star and lover of the early 1900s, Lou Tellegen, had this to say: "She was very slender and not tall; they called her *fausse maigre*, but she had a queenly carriage. Her spine was marvelously carried, so that when she stood, her back straight and her head thrown backward, she looked nearly as tall as I."

ful. She holds herself well, and her enunciation is perfectly clear. That's all that can be said for her at the moment." Her second debut, in Scribe's *Valérie*, evoked very little comment. But her third, in Molière's *Les Femmes savantes*, inspired Sarcey to write, "This performance was a very poor business. . . . That Mlle Bernhardt should be insignificant doesn't really matter very much—she's a debutante, and among the number presented to us every year it's only natural that some should be failures." Her mother's reaction to these negative remarks? "See! The whole world calls you stupid, and the whole world knows that you're my child!"

According to Thérèse Berton, Sarah took poison that night, and "For five days she hovered between life and death. . . . Asked the reason for this strange and terrible act, she answered: 'Life was useless; I wanted to see what death was like.'" More likely, she just cried herself to sleep.

In the ordinary way of things, Sarah's career at the Français would have lurched forward until she either faded out or eventually found her footing as a major player. But things didn't proceed in the ordinary way. One of Sarah's strongest attachments was to her little sister Régine, who from the start was a difficult child: stubborn, demanding, with a violent temper. She, too, suffered from Youle's lack of affection—it was always and only Jeanne, the middle sister, whom Youle cared about. But Régine attached herself passionately to Sarah, who looked after her lovingly and would often let her tag along to the theater.

Every year on Molière's birthday the entire company came forward onto the stage to salute the bust of the great writer. "It was to be my first appearance at a 'ceremony'; and my little sister . . . begged me to take her along." In the wings, as Sarah waited to go on, Régine accidentally stepped on the train of an important elderly actress, Mme Nathalie, who whipped around and slammed her against a marble pillar. Régine was crying and bleeding. "You miserable bitch," Sarah shouted, and slapped Nathalie hard on both cheeks. Swoons, tumult, laughter.

The inevitable happened. Nathalie, a senior *sociétaire*, the highest rank an actor at the Français could achieve, demanded abject apologies. Sarah refused to apologize at all: "Let her apologize to my sister first." Threats from the management, intransigence from Sarah, and a few days later she stormed out of the theater, tearing up her contract. In March 1863, eight months after her debut, Sarah Bernhardt, having performed in four plays without distinction, was gone from the Comédie-Française, and wouldn't be back for almost ten years.

But if she had lost her job, she had overnight become the object of excited notoriety in the Paris theater world, transformed from a nobody into a scandalous topic of conversation and speculation. It was the first publicity coup of her career—the first of many.

VII

ALMOST AT once she was offered a new engagement, this one through the connections of her despised godfather, M. Régis. It was at the Gymnase, a fashionable "boulevard" theater which specialized in high-life drama and comedy. During her year there she appeared in about half a dozen productions, either as an understudy or in inconsequential roles in inconsequential plays, in the last of which—*Un Mari qui lance sa femme* (A husband who launches his wife)—she played a minor comic character, the Russian Princess Dimchinka. (Youle: "You were ridiculous. I was very upset.") The next day, after the usual sleepless night, she impulsively sneaked out of the house with a neighbor's maid for companion and, leaving behind a note for her mother and an incoherent letter for the management of the Gymnase—"Have pity on a poor crazy girl!"—rushed off to Spain, where she took in the sights and enjoyed herself thoroughly until she rushed back to Paris on hearing that her mother was very ill.

Arriving home, she found Youle recovering from a severe attack of pleurisy. It's at this point in *My Double Life* that she writes most tellingly and convincingly about Youle:

> She was very placid, but she was determined, and this determination of hers sometimes resulted in the most violent anger. She would turn very pale, and violet rings would appear around her eyes, her lips would tremble, her teeth chattered, her beautiful eyes took on a fixed gaze, the words would sputter from her throat, all chopped up, hissing and hoarse. Then she would faint, and the veins of her throat would swell and her hands and feet turn icy cold. Sometimes she would be unconscious for hours, and the doctors told us that she might die in one of these attacks, so that we did all in our power to avoid these terrible incidents.

"As for me," Sarah goes on, "I am not placid. I am active, and always ready for a fight, and what I want I always want immediately. I don't have the gentle obstinacy peculiar to my mother. The blood begins to boil under my temples before I have time to control it."

Two such stormy women could not easily live together, and some money that Sarah fortuitously received at this juncture from her Dutch grandmother made it possible for her to set up in her own apartment nearby, giving her the privacy that the next stage in her life would require. Little Régine, now about nine, begged Sarah to take her with her. "Take her," Youle said. "She's unbearable." Wildly kissing her mother, Régine cried, "You're glad I'm going, aren't you? Now everything can be for your Jeanne." Youle's response was to lean back against Jeanne and say, "We two will stay together." "I was completely stupefied," Sarah tells us, "and shut my eyes so that I wouldn't have to watch."

Sarah's lover the Prince de Ligne ...

Sarah's memoirs are full of her Spanish trip, but the whole thing has the feel of a story concocted to cover up certain unpalatable truths. Since her son, Maurice, was born on December 22, 1864 (she was twenty), she may well have been aware of her pregnancy in April when she fled the Gymnase. (In the memoirs, by the way, Maurice is not mentioned until he's four.) But who was Maurice's father?

Although Sarah liked to joke that it was this or that unlikely person (Victor Hugo, General Boulanger, even the Duke of Clarence, who, as one of her biographers points out, was born in 1864—the same year as Maurice himself), she let it be known that it was really the handsome young Belgian Prince de Ligne. He, like all her lovers, is not identified in her memoirs, or even

and their (presumed) son, Maurice Bernhardt

mentioned, but she always implied that he was the great love of her life. The conflicting narratives she offered about how they met and how their relationship developed are all dubious, but it would seem that they really did meet, quickly entering into the liaison that produced Maurice.

Louis Verneuil reports his grandmother-in-law spinning a tale so romantic and improbable that it's impossible to credit it. Sarah, as a member of the Gymnase, is assisting at a private reading at the Tuileries palace and embarrasses herself and the Gymnase by reciting a poem by Victor Hugo before the emperor. Either she didn't know or didn't care that he had banished the great poet to Guernsey for his republican views.

The royal party exits in a huff, and Sarah is being severely admonished by the theater's director, who grabs her by the wrist, causing her to emit "a cry of rage and pain." A man's voice is heard from the back of the room: "Kindly leave that child alone." The director: "Why don't you mind your own business, sir? First of all, who are you?" The hero: "I am Prince Henri de Ligne. I will not allow a woman to be insulted in my presence, especially a young woman who is pretty, naïve, and defenseless, like this young lady." And one thing leads to another.

"They met the next day and the day after . . . every day and every night until the summer. This great love soon grew into a veritable passion which was sincere on both sides, the rarest and most touching reciprocal feeling which ever united two young hearts." The young prince is sent abroad by the Belgian government, and when he returns he can't immediately locate Sarah—she's ordered everyone to withhold her address should anyone ask for her. "She was extremely proud, and nothing in the world would have made her appear to be taking advantage of her approaching maternity." But love will have its way, and well after the birth of Maurice, the prince manages to track her down, and "their passion was resumed as ardently as before, but more profoundly, more seriously." Indeed, "their life together was unusually and sublimely beautiful," and he decides to marry her.

His noble family, naturally, intervenes, with a cousin of Henri's traveling to Paris and ringing Sarah's doorbell. When she considers the consequences to Henri of his marrying her, she makes the supreme sacrifice and dismisses him. "But when the young prince had gone—forever—she fell on the floor in a faint. A violent fever seized her poor frail body and, for nearly a month, Mme Guérard and her family feared for her life."

Did she really tell all this to Verneuil? If so, she told a very different story to his wife, Lysiane.

In this somewhat more believable account, on the very night of the Princess Dimchinka debacle, Dumas, to cheer her up, strongly recommends that she get out of Paris at once. ("In ten minutes, Dumas had fastened wings on the little Bernhardt, awakening in her the desire for travel which is innate in every child of the Jewish race.") The next morning he escorts her and Mme Guérard to Brussels, entrusting her well-being to friends of his. In no time, she's off to a costume ball, and there—got up as Queen Elizabeth—she encounters a dashing figure dressed as Hamlet. Meaningful glances through their masks; flirtatious badinage. When they encounter each other the next day, without benefit of costumes, sparks fly—*et voilà*, Maurice.

The scenario that follows runs parallel to the Verneuil version and borrows from the supposed Spanish escapade: Youle desperately ill, Sarah back to Paris. Henri follows her, hopes to marry her, but it is not to be, although Verneuil tells us in extenuation that "the part he played in the life of Sarah Bernhardt was always particularly knightly, loyal, and generous. After sixty years her memory of him was full of tenderness and gratitude."

Even as the prince is pursuing her in Paris (they're dining in the same restaurant), Sarah hears that her apartment is going up in flames, and she falls forward, unconscious. Later that night, Guérard remarks that fainting this way is unlike her. Pressed to reveal the truth, "Sarah put her lips close to her friend's ear, and Mme Guérard went through a series of emotions. At first she was terrified, then delighted, then she wept. 'Heavens! What are you going to do?' 'Work! Work! Live for my art and for the little child that is soon to be born. Oh no! Don't be sorry for me. I am happy! Happy!'" Curtain.

Both these tales, though so different in specifics, no doubt helped Lysiane consider the circumstances of her father's birth in the rosiest possible light. They also must have satisfied Sarah's need to think of herself as having enjoyed a beautiful, ill-fated love affair on the highest social level. A prince, ready to marry her! An impeccable aristocratic background for her adored Maurice! Heroic self-sacrifice! Remember: By the time

Sarah spun these fantasies of a noble if somewhat irregularly situated young woman giving up her happiness for the sake of the upper-class man she loves, she had played the heroine of *La Dame aux camélias* more than three thousand times.

As usual, Marie Colombier supplies a corrective. Sarah is walking desultorily through the Tuileries, considering how she can improve her fortunes, and *regardez:* "A man of elegant appearance and aristocratic mien, who with a glass in one eye, was calmly ogling her." Can this be the Prince Charming she's been dreaming of? Five minutes later they're sitting next to each other on a bench; half an hour later they depart as close friends. The man is the "Prince de Dygne, a fantastic swell who prided himself on hunting up someone original to love and dispensing his gallantries in every part of the world." A quiet dinner is proposed and agreed to.

They meet once a week or so until she makes the frightful discovery that she's going to become a mother. Going straight to the prince's new mansion, where he's hosting a housewarming party, she sends in her card and he comes out to greet her. Her news doesn't go down well, and she starts to make a scene. At last, writes Colombier, Dygne loses patience and grows hard and cutting. "My young friend," he says, "since you belong to the theater, ask that distinguished actress Augustine Brohan to give you the benefit of her advice. She's a very agreeable lady and she'll treat you to one of her cleverest witticisms: 'When you sit down on a bundle of thorns, you can't tell which one of them is pricking you.'" And with a laugh he goes back to his guests.

But Sarah isn't laughing. She goes half-mad, and not only at his rejection of her and the child. What's tormenting her, Colombier gloats, is a touch of doubt. During her days of want, she had visited "certain hospitable institutions." Could it be that "in one of these discreet asylums she had contracted her present infirmity?" This implication that she had made herself available in bordellos was one of Colombier's most savage thrusts.

VIII

EVEN SO, her amorous life was proceeding far more successfully than her professional life. Beginning in April 1864 when she abandoned the Gymnase, she had no work in the theater for more than two years, except for a short run as a replacement in a kind of fairy spectacle called *La Biche au bois*. So far she had made no impression at all as an actress. What was she doing, and what was she living on?

At first, according to Thérèse Berton, she "was a member of one of the fastest sets of a fast city. . . . Her health was bad, she had frequent spells of coughing, and the tell-tale flush of fever was constantly on her cheeks." With her sister Jeanne, who was only fourteen, she would turn up at public balls and "somewhat questionable entertainments in the homes of titled acquaintances." Only a miracle, says Berton, could have saved her from the fate of countless pretty, improvident, and immoral young women. "But the needful miracle happened": motherhood, although not until she had (barely) survived a difficult *accouchement*. Her love for Maurice fired in her a determination to work and succeed that she had previously lacked. "Every aim of her existence was to provide for him while he was young the shield of respectability she herself had never known."

With only two hundred francs to her name, she told Berton, and that meager sum soon to be gone, she wrote to Ligne appealing for assistance and imploring him to take pity on her and their child. "The prince's reply was brutality itself: 'I know a woman named Bernhardt,' he wrote, 'but I do not know her child.'" And he enclosed a fifty-franc note! It's at that point, according to Berton, that Sarah goes to Ligne's house and is cuttingly rejected. Well, it's a good scene, and does it really matter whether it happened before or after Maurice was born?

This period in her life has been fudged over by her first biographers, starting with herself, but it's now clear that she was living by her wits—and her body. Not, of course, as a common prostitute or kept woman, but in a unique situation that she fashioned through her sexuality, her charm, and her common sense. In the white-satin salon of her new apartment in the rue Duphot she managed to establish a kind of court, made up of a group of distinguished men who were seemingly content to pay joint homage (and a fairly allocated tariff) to her while sharing her favors openly and with equanimity. "What's odd," she told Colombier—if you can believe Colombier, and in this case I do—"is how well they get along together. They never quarrel and they seem to adore one another. I sometimes think that if I were to disappear, my menagerie would go on congregating in my apartment with the greatest of pleasure." Apparently, among their joint ventures was chipping in to buy Sarah the elaborate coffin she had always wanted, and which famously accompanied her thereafter wherever she went.

Among her gentlemen friends during these years was Marshal Canrobert, an important and venerated figure in the regime; the vicomte Olympe Aguado, an immensely rich Spaniard, who eventually moved on to Jeanne; the equally rich Khalil Bey, an Egyptian diplomat and art collector; an industrialist, Robert de Brimont; two central figures in the journalism of the day, Émile de Girardin and Arthur Meyer (who would remain a friend for life); the banker Jacques Stern, who would later marry her friend and rival Sophie Croizette; and the Marquis de Caux, who would marry the great opera star Adelina Patti.

Colombier happily recounts some of the tricks Sarah employed to extract extra money from her "stockholders"—for instance, arranging to be discovered with blood on a handkerchief held up to her mouth. (She would puncture her gums with a needle.) Marie's malice by this point in her chronicle seems almost out of control—she's particularly vicious about what she implies was the pimping of Jeanne and, later, Régine—but there's no way she can ignore the change for the better in Sarah's professional circumstances which took place in the summer of 1866.

IX

THE ODÉON was France's second official theater, after the Comédie-Française, and was therefore under the overall supervision of the head of the theater division of the Ministère des Beaux-Arts—that family friend Camille Doucet, who was always ready to help Sarah. In mid-1866, desperate to work, she wrote to him for an appointment, and the next day he welcomed her at the ministry. "Now listen, you terrible child, you've got to calm down and stop wasting your talents. No more rushing around and running away and slapping people. So let's see how we can fix things up." Taking a letter out of a drawer, he went on, "Maybe this will do the trick!" and told Sarah that he had just been approached by the new directors of the Odéon, Charles de Chilly and Félix Duquesnel, who were asking for new artists to fill out the company roster. "Yes, we're going to make this work!" And several days later, he summoned her to the ministry again to tell her that Duquesnel was expecting her to call on him. "It hasn't been easy, though," he told her. "Everyone knows how hard you are to control, and I've had to swear you'll be as gentle as a lamb." Sarah gave him every assurance that she would be, and went home to dress for the occasion.

Twenty-eight years later, Duquesnel wrote about their meeting:

> One day my chambermaid entered my room in a panic
> and said "Monsieur, monsieur, there's a Chinese
> lady here who's insisting on seeing you!" I was intrigued,
> since I had no relations in the Middle Kingdom, and
> I had her usher in "the Chinese lady." There stood the
> most adorable creature imaginable—Sarah Bernhardt
> in all the glory of her youth. She wasn't just pretty, she
> was more dangerous than that. She was dressed in a pale
> crêpe de chine blouse with shiny embroidery, cut in
> some Chinese style that left her bare arms and shoulders

lightly covered in lace. There was a small feathered fan at her waist, and on her head she had a coolie hat made of finely woven straw, hung with beads that trembled when she moved. Her maid was with her, carrying a beautiful pink and white baby in her arms—Maurice Bernhardt. Our interview was very quick—we understood each other immediately. I felt that I was face to face with a marvelously gifted creature of rare intelligence and limitless energy and willpower hidden behind her delicate appearance. She was everything that was entrancing and seductive as a woman; artistry emanated from her entire being. All she needed was to be started off in the right direction and be exposed to the public. As for her voice, it was pure as crystal. It went straight to the heart, like heavenly music.

Sarah's account of this fateful meeting? "A young man appeared, looking very elegant. He was smiling and altogether charming. I couldn't grasp the fact that this fair-haired, gay young man was going to be my new manager." (She would grasp it—and him—soon enough.) Meanwhile, to conclude the formalities she had to proceed to the Odéon to meet his co-manager, Chilly, with whom she had had an unfortunate run-in some months earlier. He kept her waiting, he was rude, and after signing her contract he said, "You know, it's Duquesnel who's responsible for your being here. There's no way I would have taken you on." Her reply: "And if it had been you alone, monsieur, I wouldn't have signed. So we're even."

No matter. Three years after her inglorious departure from the Comédie-Française she was at last on the right path. It was at the popular Odéon—that far more easygoing and re-laxed theater—that she came into her own, revealing for the first time her enormous talent and conquering both the critics and the public. Camille Doucet's intervention with the young Duquesnel proved to be the gateway to her amazing career.

Sarah's double debut at the Odéon, on August 15,

1866, however, was hardly auspicious—she was unsuited to Marivaux's witty comedy *Le Jeu de l'amour et du hasard* and made a poor impression in a horrible costume as Aricie in *Phèdre*. Chilly gloated and demanded that she be let go at the end of her monthlong trial period, but Duquesnel persisted, and backed his judgment by surreptitiously giving the theater one hundred francs a month to cover the cost of keeping Sarah on.

Over the next months she acted a variety of roles, mostly classical ingénues, and it wasn't until she had worked for almost a year that she scored her first success, in Racine's *Athalie*. She was playing the ten-year-old boy Zacharie, and some students from the Conservatoire were to recite the choruses. At rehearsal they were doing such a terrible job that Chilly interrupted: "Let the little one speak all the choruses. That should work, given her pretty voice." It *did* work. Everyone applauded, Duquesnel hid his smile, and "the first performance was a veritable small triumph for me! Oh, quite a small one, but still full of promise for my future. The public, charmed with the sweetness of my voice and its crystal purity, encored the spoken choruses, and I was rewarded by three bursts of applause." Even before this, though, her hard work had begun attracting enthusiastic attention from the critics. The all-important Sarcey had written of one performance, "Mlle Bernhardt astonished me!" and went on to praise her singularly perfect intonation, her elegance, and her remarkable stage presence. And to note how natural and unself-conscious she seemed.

Seven months after *Athalie*, a more substantial success: as Anna Damby in a revival of Dumas' *Kean*. The Odéon had announced a revival of Victor Hugo's famous *Ruy Blas*, a barely masked cry for political reform, but had been ordered by the government to cancel it. The management substituted *Kean*, and the opening night began with a violent protest by antimonarchist students from the nearby Sorbonne, radical in their politics then as now and always ready to demonstrate. They also didn't like it that Dumas' unpopular mistress was in his box with him. "We want *Ruy Blas*! We want *Ruy Blas*!" Dumas was mortified and shaken. When the play finally got under way, the actors could hardly be heard until, at her entrance, Sarah—though herself extremely frightened—strode downstage and shouted that if the students were so dedicated to justice, it was hardly just of them to blame Dumas for the banning of *Ruy Blas*.

She was already becoming a favorite of these fiery young people—they were starting to call themselves the *Saradoteurs*—and they settled down to listen, and were delighted and moved by her performance. Sarah had turned a disaster into a success: As *Le Figaro* put it, "She tamed the public like a little Orpheus." And Chilly not only gave back to Duquesnel the money he had paid out to cover her salary but gave Sarah a raise. From then on they addressed each other with the familiar *tu* and, as Sarah put it, "became the best possible friends."

Sarah's Kean was Charles Berton, the father of Pierre and father-in-law of Thérèse, who perversely insisted that it was the son (her husband) who played Kean. Both Bertons were at the Odéon, and perhaps it was at this time that Sarah inaugurated her lifelong habit of automatically sleeping with her leading men. As one of her biographers tells us, "Sarah preferred to satisfy her caprices with her colleagues in a dressing room, after a performance. At this period she was credited with both Bertons, the father and the son."

Pierre, Thérèse tells us, "confessed to me in later life after our marriage that 'the days that Sarah Bernhardt devoted to me were like pages from immortality. One felt that one could not die!'" She goes on to say, however, "I have always doubted whether she gave to Pierre that full and sincere depth of passion he brought to her. Sarah's was a nature too complex to harbor any deep feeling for long." But then Thérèse Berton is inevitably unreliable, given her double mission: undercutting Sarah's reputation while exalting her late husband's importance.

The revival of *Kean* took place in February 1868. It was

almost a year later, after succeeding in several other roles (including an affecting Cordelia) that she found the play and the part that were to bring her stardom. The play was a one-act, two-character vehicle called *Le Passant* (The Passerby). The author was François Coppée, a young civil servant with no track record, who happened to be the lover of a highly regarded older actress at the Odéon, Mme Agar, with whom Sarah was on very good terms. One day Agar asked Sarah to read a new verse drama by Coppée, with the idea that she would play the young Renaissance troubadour named Zanetto who "passes by" one night, though not before enjoying an interlude with the aging courtesan, Silvia, whom he encounters in her Florentine garden. Zanetto would be Sarah's first significant trouser role; the beautiful, womanly Agar would, of course, be Silvia.

According to Sarah, she read *Le Passant* on her way home from the theater and turned back, finding Duquesnel just about to leave. "Read this, please." "I'll take it with me." "Oh, no, read it here at once! Shall I read it to you?" "No, no, your voice is treacherous. It can make lovely poetry out of the stupidest lines." But he agreed to read it (to himself) on the spot, and when he finished he exclaimed, "It's delicious. It's a perfect masterpiece!" And they agreed to try it out at once, at a benefit performance, with scenery from a recent failure and costumes that Sarah and Agar would have to pay for themselves. (Needless to say, there are other versions of how Sarah and Agar wheedled *Le Passant* onto the stage.)

It was the first really great triumph of Sarah's career, the performance that overnight made her the most talked-about young actress in Paris. She and Agar played it 140 times, and when Agar wasn't available, Sarah played it opposite Marie Colombier, still her close friend. Today, *Le Passant* seems overly precious in its flowery romanticism, but that was the exact quality that appealed to the jaded audience of the moment. Sarah's charming presence in her minstrel costume and the beauty of

Marie Agar

her delivery of Coppée's pretty lines conquered the public, and the critics as well. (The influential poet and critic Théodore de Banville: "She recited verse the way nightingales sing, the way the wind sighs, the way brooks murmur . . . ")

The climax of *Le Passant*'s trajectory of triumph came with a command performance at the Tuileries palace before the emperor and empress. Sarah had already met Napoléon III and had come to admire him, or at least his looks: She felt that he resembled his great predecessor—and Sarah had a weakness for the Napoleonic look. It's probable that at some point the emperor and the actress indulged each other's penchant for sexual adventure, just as Sarah later would have a special relationship combining romance and mutual admiration with Edward, Prince of Wales.

As we have seen, Sarah—forgetting her early disdain for her mother's career— had no problem with sharing her favors. It was during these first years at the Odéon that she took up

Pierre Berton

with one of the most distinguished men of her time, the ul-trafashionable Charles Haas, who was not only elegant, hand-some, and sophisticated but was socially impeccable: one of the very few Jewish members of the Jockey Club and accepted by the aristocracy of the Faubourg St. Germain—*le gratin.* Among his close friends: Degas and the Prince of Wales. In the 1860s he was famous for his worldliness and his success with women; today he is remembered only as Sarah's lover and as the direct model for Proust's Charles Swann. (Sarah, of course, was to be the model for Proust's Berma.)

The letters that Sarah wrote to Haas at this time make it clear that he is the adored one, she the adorer. "I love you. I know perfectly well that you don't return my love but please behave as though you did. Dear friend, come to me at three o'clock. It would give me so much pleasure." "Thank you for your letters, my dear love. Above all, thank you for your visits." "Come back as soon as possible, dear Charles. I long to see you.

. . . My hand, all my being goes out to you." When he ended their liaison, tactfully paying her off, she wrote, "I accept, but only if it's a loan. Thank you, dear friend, thank you." And they stayed friends until he died, in 1902. Indeed, staying on the best of terms with ex-lovers was one of Sarah's extracurricular talents.

It was while Sarah was dining with Haas and Arthur Meyer that her apartment went up in flames—a nursemaid had been careless with the candles. In some reports, the three friends are at a restaurant (the Prince de Ligne, as we have seen, at a nearby table); in others, they're at her home when the fire breaks out, and she rushes upstairs to collect baby Maurice, wake the servants, and carry her old and disagreeable Dutch grandmother, who's living with her, down the stairs. Unfortunately, but not untypically, Sarah had forgotten to sign her insurance contract and she was ruined and homeless, temporarily moving in with Youle.

Duquesnel came to the rescue, organizing a gala benefit to help her start up again, and to the surprise of many, the volunteer star of the evening was Adelina Patti, the most adored singer of her time. As we may remember, Patti had married the Marquis de Caux, one of Sarah's former "stockholders," and he persuaded his wife to come to the aid of his former mistress. Or was there a touch of blackmail involved? In any event, the evening was a huge success, Sarah was solvent again, and life resumed, her career uninterrupted.

Two more successes followed swiftly: *Le Bâtard*, a defense of illegitimacy, which not only saw the Bertons, father and son, playing rival brothers, but had in minor roles two of Sarah's future lovers and leading men: Mounet-Sully and Édouard Angelo. George Sand's *L'Autre* followed, again with the Bertons, but this time as father and son. In her memoirs, Sarah speaks warmly of Sand ("She was a sweet, charming creature, extremely timid. . . . I used to watch her with the most romantic affection. . . . I used to sit down by her, and when I took her hand in mine I held it as long as possible"), but Sand's journals tell a different story: "They're all doing well except Sarah. She's a good girl, but definitely stupid." "In many ways Sarah is stupid, but she has a pleasing nature." "Sarah and Berton absent. Jeanne [Bernhardt] had a miscarriage." "Mlle Sarah kept us waiting. She doesn't really give a damn about her sister, hasn't worked, and interprets her role like the great tart she is." "I'm afraid Mlle Sarah is cuckoo, but everyone says she's going to be fine." "All the acting has improved, especially Sarah's. . . . At last she's identified with the young, honest, and interesting character she's playing." The critic Théophile Gautier: "Young and charming, Bernhardt projects the chaste and audacious quality of a real girl who knows nothing, fears nothing, and reproaches herself with nothing." Which sounds a good deal like Sarah herself.

Sarah's career was in full stride now, four years after her arrival at the Odéon. But it was 1870, and in July of that year the emperor declared war on Germany. The disastrous Franco-Prussian war that followed would temporarily halt her artistic progress, but it would also have the extraordinary side effect of turning her into an offstage heroine—the first step in her unlikely transformation from headstrong girl with dubious morals to national icon.

X

SARAH DEVOTED as much as fifteen percent of her memoirs to her war experiences. There were countless dramatic scenes to narrate and embroider (she's writing almost thirty-five years after the event), and there's a remarkable energy and zest to her prose as she describes the frightful things she witnessed and participated in. You can tell that for all the horrors, the war excited her, and so did her role in it.

She was in the south of France on a rest cure in July 1870

when the emperor went to war, and along with thousands of others she was frantic to get back to Paris. Arriving home, she was soon faced with the disaster of the French campaign, climaxed by the emperor's surrender of eighty thousand men and his sword at Sedan in September. Soon the Germans were approaching the capital to lay siege to it, and Sarah was determined to get her entire family out of the city and to safety. Having bullied their way onto a train to Holland, she returned to her apartment and prepared to help her country. Although, as she says, "I hate war! It exasperates me and makes me shudder from head to foot," it never occurred to her to run from it. Instead, "I decided to use my strength and intelligence in tending the wounded."

As wounded soldiers stream into the city, she receives permission from Duquesnel to requisition the Odéon (it had closed its doors) and from the War Office to open a military hospital there. At once she begins laying in provisions, calling on her friends and acquaintances everywhere to help. Crucial

assistance comes from the new prefect of the Seine, who, when she goes to see him, turns out to be her old lover the comte de Keratry—the hussar. Not that she acknowledges him as such: To her readers she refers to him as a young lieutenant she had once met at her Aunt Rosine's and who had introduced her to his mother ("a very charming woman"), at whose soirées Sarah had recited poetry.

What a surprise to come upon him again under these circumstances! "I never thought it was you I was coming to see, and I'm delighted, because you're going to let me have everything I ask for. . . . I have five wounded men already, and more are on their way." Gallant as ever, he replies, "Well, give me your orders, madame," and soon he has sent her ten barrels of wine and two of brandy; thirty thousand eggs packed in boxes; a hundred bags of coffee, crates of tea, forty boxes of biscuits, a thousand tins of preserves, and more. She spots his superb fur-lined coat, and she takes that too: "I shall need a great many overcoats, and this one looks extremely warm." Laughing, he hands it over, only asking, "Will you allow me to keep my muffler?" (This is certainly a good story, so why ask whether it's a true one?)

Other friends came through with other essentials. A chocolate manufacturer sent five hundred pounds of chocolate; a flour dealer sent twenty sacks of flour; others, sardines, lentils, sugar, butter, nightshirts, and sheets; and "I bought up a job lot of two hundred flannel vests." She emptied out the theater to make room for beds and cots; moved her cook in to deal with meals; and organized one of the older actresses, Mme Lambquin, as well as Marie Colombier (whose participation, not surprisingly, goes unmentioned in Sarah's memoirs) and of course Mme Guérard, as her chief aides. As the siege of Paris took hold, Sarah's military hospital was ready.

There was a genuine need. The injured, the maimed, the dying flooded in. Sarah had them in the lobbies, in the auditorium, in the wings, in the dressing rooms, on the stage. Fifty, sixty, one hundred . . . and she tended them herself, sleeping in the theater, nursing the men, providing care and solace—and autographing pictures (one, apparently, for a young soldier named Foch, who would one day command the armies of France).

Yes, it was a role she was playing, as Colombier snidely remarks, but it was a role she believed in. Always, Sarah was a patriot, and always when she decided something needed to be done, she was happiest doing it herself. Nothing fazed her.

> The bombardment of Paris continued. One night the Brothers from the École Chrétienne came to ask us for conveyances and help, in order to collect the dead on the Chatillon Plateau. I let them have my two conveyances, and I went with them to the battlefield. Ah, what a horrible memory! It was like a scene from Dante! It was an icy-cold night and we could hardly move forward. Finally, by the light of torches and lanterns we saw that we had arrived. I got out of the vehicle with the infirmary attendant and his assistant. We had to go slowly, as at every step we were treading on the dying or the dead. We passed along murmuring: "Ambulance! Ambulance!" When we heard a groan we turned our steps in the direction from which it came. Ah, the first man that I found in this way! He was half lying down, his body supported by a heap of the dead. I raised my lantern to look at his face and found that his ear and part of his jaw had been blown off. Great clots of blood, coagulated by the cold, hung from his lower jaw. There was a wild look in his eyes. I took a wisp of straw, dipped it in my flask, drew up a few drops of brandy and blew them into the poor fellow's mouth between his teeth. I repeated this three times. A little life then came back to him and we took him away in one of the vehicles. . . . There were so many wounded that it was impossible to transport them all, and I sobbed at the thought of my helplessness.

Surely this has the ring of truth.

As the siege went on and the shelling grew more intense,

it became evident that the Odéon was too identifiable a target for the German gunners. Sarah moved her patients to the cellars, then sent the worst cases to the Val-de-Grâce Hospital and rented a big apartment for the twenty or so who were convalescent. She herself was exhausted, barely a skeleton. But she had done something big, and everyone knew it. She had conceived a plan and executed it with formidable concentration, reaching out to her entire world of the rich and the powerful and organizing it to help her achieve her goal. She had given of herself with unflagging energy, and she had shown herself—and everyone else—what she was capable of.

During the siege, she had been without word of her family in Holland—not just six-year-old Maurice but her mother, Jeanne and Régine, Jeanne's baby, her aunts—except for one or two brief messages delivered through the United States minister (he had stayed on in Paris, which was otherwise cut off from the world). "Everyone well. Courage. A thousand kisses. Your mother." This uncharacteristically warm communication from Youle may have assuaged Sarah's immediate anxieties, but when the final collapse came and the humiliating armistice was signed at the end of January 1871, she learned to her mortification and fury that the family had moved from The Hague, where she had believed they were in residence, to the luxurious German spa of Homburg-von-der-Hoehe, near Frankfurt, where Rosine had friends. This not only went against Sarah's patriotic hatred of the Germans but exacerbated her sensitivity about her ancestry—of being labeled by her enemies as German.

Instantly she accosted Adolphe Thiers—"chief of executive power" and soon to be president—for permission to cross the barely pacified battle lines and go in search of the family and bring them home. Unlike her account of the siege, her narrative of her eleven-day trek across France and into Germany reads like a thriller: danger at every turn, hideous conditions, mounting anxiety and exhaustion, with no companions except Maurice's young governess—and a revolver. Indefatigable as always, she managed to shepherd herself and the entire family back through the recent war zone—eleven people in all. But within weeks she was to find herself in danger of being arrested when Paris fell into the grip of the Commune uprising—that terrifying moment in 1871, in the wake of the defeat, when the working class defied the new national government and sealed off Paris from the rest of the country, resulting in siege warfare, street-to-street fighting, hostages, executions, before the national government finally prevailed.

Sarah was in no way a political radical, and although she claimed to be a fervent republican (apart from her weakness for the Napoleonic emperors), in fact she was hardly political at all, beyond her personal connections to various important figures in various governments; but then everything with her was personal. She was dismayed by the violence that the outbreak had unleashed, and since the theaters were still closed, she moved out of the city to nearby St. Germain-en-Laye, from which, standing on the heights, she "could see the flames rising, proud and destructive." (These were the flames that destroyed the Hôtel de Ville, along with the records of her birth.) By then she had attached to herself a certain Captain O'Connor, an idyll that lost much of its charm when, one day while they were out riding, he shot down a Communard in cold blood. The handsome O'Connor was fighting on the side of the government, which had fled Paris and was installed in nearby Versailles. Sarah had poached him from her sister Régine while remaining the official and well-compensated mistress of the rich banker Jacques Stern. Money had to come from somewhere.

By the end of May, the uprising had been bloodily suppressed—it had lasted exactly two months—with tens of thousands dead on both sides, partly through the battles in the streets, partly through executions. "At last we were able to go back to Paris. The abominable and shameful peace with Germany had been signed and the wretched Commune crushed. Everything was supposed to be in order again. But what blood and ashes! what women in mourning! what ruins! The bitter odor of smoke was what we inhaled in Paris."

With the theaters reopened, it wasn't long before Sarah was summoned to rehearsals at the Odéon. A series of plays— some successful, some not—occupied her during the next months, but she tells us that although she had just enjoyed a particular success in a play opposite her old friend Paul Porel, "I was awaiting the event which was to consecrate me a star. I did not quite know what I was expecting, but I knew that my Messiah had to come. And it was the greatest poet of the century who was to place on my head the crown of the Elect."

XI

THE POET, of course, was Victor Hugo, who had returned, a hero, from his nineteen years of exile in the Channel Islands. Now the empire was gone, replaced by a republic, and to the elation of his countrymen Hugo, widely considered the greatest man of his time, was back in Paris. The Odéon had decided to present the revival of *Ruy Blas* that had been replaced by *Kean* back in 1868, and Sarah was determined to play the romantic Spanish queen, Doña Marie de Neubourg. Organizing friends of Hugo's to support her candidacy, she was awarded the role and was asked to come to the poet's home the next day at two o'clock for a first reading of the play. Offended by this somewhat irregular request—first readings ordinarily took place on the stage—and encouraged by her "little court," she listened to her old friend Marshal Canrobert and sent the following letter to the poet: "Monsieur, the Queen has taken a chill and her lady-in-waiting forbids her to go out. You know better that anyone else the etiquette of this Spanish Court. Pity your Queen, Monsieur." His reply: "I am your servant, Madame."

Victor Hugo

Almost at once she realized how she had misjudged him, and quickly came to revere him. Rehearsals were a pleasure—Hugo himself was directing—and on the opening night, February 19, 1872, Sarah had the greatest triumph of her career to date. Backstage, mobbed by admirers, "breathless, dazed, and yet delighted by my success," Sarah suddenly saw the crowd separating and forming two lines, and caught a glimpse of Hugo coming toward her. "In a second all the stupid ideas I had had about this immense genius flashed through my mind. . . . At that moment, when my life was spreading its wings, I should have liked to cry out to him in repentance, and to tell him of my devout gratitude. Before I could speak, though, he was down on his knee and, raising my hands to his lips, he murmured 'Thank you! Thank you!' . . . He was so handsome that night, with his wide forehead, which seemed to retain the light, his thick, silvery fleece of hair, and his laughing luminous eyes."

Hugo was seventy, Sarah was twenty-seven. *Quand même.* They both had spectacular amorous histories, and it is assumed that they now shared another one. Hugo's journals record various encounters. The day after the opening: "Saw and congratulated Sarah Bernhardt. She said to me, Kiss me. Bise de boca." ("Kiss on the mouth." He always noted romantic encounters in Spanish.) Their friendship continued for several years. As late as November 1875, Hugo was confiding to his journal "S. B. No sera el chico hecho." ("There isn't going to be a baby.") And Sarah was writing to her doctor about a trip to England, "The voyage is on again; the real reason is fear of trouble in regard to Victor Hugo. I'm ill, I'm exhausted . . . and I'm irritated by the stupid egotism of men." As one French biographer speculated, could Hugo's entry in his journal be a sigh of relief? False alarm! No "chico"!

The author of *Ruy Blas* was not the only one enraptured by Sarah in his play; the critics were as well. Sarcey: "No role was ever better adapted to Mlle Sarah Bernhardt's talents than that of this melancholy queen." It was her voice, her enchanting delivery of Hugo's poetry, that captivated him. Overnight, Sarah had achieved her ambition and been acclaimed the finest actress in Paris.

Given all the acclaim, it was clear that the Comédie-Française could no longer ignore her, and the critics—led by Sarcey, whose influence on the company was immense—were pushing the theater to invite her back. (Who knows the extent to which Sarah was behind the scenes, encouraging them to push?)

One day a letter arrived from Émile Perrin, the head of

the Français, asking her to call on him. Sarah's version is that she immediately went to Duquesnel, showed him the letter, and asked for a raise. According to her, he advised her to stay at the Odéon and promised to confer with Chilly about money. (She was demanding 15,000 francs a year, as opposed to the 12,500 she could get from Perrin.) Chilly balked: There was a year to go on her contract, why should he release her? On hearing this, Sarah jumped up and rushed straight to Perrin to sign. When she showed her new contract to Duquesnel, he said, "in a grave, hurt voice: 'You should never have done that without telling me first. It shows a lack of confidence, and I don't deserve that.'" Even Sarah was chagrined. "I excused myself in as poor a way as possible to Duquesnel. He was hurt, and I was a little ashamed, for this man had given me nothing but proofs of kindness. It was he, after all, who despite Chilly's resistance had opened the door to my future."

As he had threatened to do, Chilly, in a rage, sued her and won his case—Sarah was ordered to pay six thousand francs in damages to the management of the Odéon. Meanwhile, Hugo hosted a dinner to celebrate the hundredth performance of *Ruy Blas*, and in the midst of the speeches and congratulations Chilly was felled by a stroke. He died soon thereafter, "causing me intense grief." Possibly.

The prestige of the Comédie-Française and the higher salary, plus the satisfaction at being wooed back after her ignominious rout nine years before, made Sarah's decision to return there a certainty, and the comedy of her back-and-forth with Duquesnel and Chilly over money is a typical example of her eternal need to justify her behavior. But she knew even then what she was giving up. "I left the Odéon with very great respect, for I adored and still adore that theater. . . . My mind never goes back to those few years of my life without a childish emotion." This was where she had mastered her art and discovered how to command the critics and the public. It was her learning ground and her proving ground.

But the Odéon was too small to hold her. "I felt that my life of hoping and dreaming was to come to an end here. I felt that the way was open for the fruition of all my dreams; that life was about to commence." She also knew what she was getting into. "I understood that I was going back into the lion's den." Not everyone, however, saw it that way. Théodore de Banville put it most famously: "Sarah Bernhardt's engagement at the Théâtre Français is a revolution. Poetry has entered the domain of dramatic art. Or, if you like, the wolf has entered the sheepfold."

XII

As an artist Sarah had evolved almost out of recognition in the nine years since she had left the theater of Molière, but the theater itself hadn't changed, except that it was looking a little more fusty and out of date. That, apart from the urgings of Sarcey and other critics, was what had impelled Perrin to invite her back. Not only was she the most interesting young actress in Paris, but she was likely to be a boon at the box office— and the Français was in a slump. No great tragic actress had come along to challenge the memory of the sublime Rachel, or to attract the public as Rachel had in her short career before dying—of tuberculosis—at the age of thirty-six.

Although, like the Odéon, the Français was a government-run theater, it was organized on a very different basis, and the atmosphere was radically different as well. New actors were brought in at a low level, and at low salaries. They were officially called *pensionnaires*. Eventually, they might become *sociétaires*, with far more money plus some kind of share in the profits. At the top of the hierarchy were the senior *sociétaires*, who in essence were secure for life. And it was the *sociétaires* themselves who elected newer actors to join their privileged ranks.

Not surprisingly, the notorious Sarah Bernhardt—the defiant rule breaker, the glutton for publicity, and the representative of a new, more realistic, more exciting approach to acting—was not a favorite among the old-timers, who remembered vividly her brief, scandalous stay there. She did, though, have a few old friends—among them Sophie Croizette and the great Coquelin, who would years later be the original Cyrano. Most of the women resented her provocative manner and felt threatened in regard to their own status and their own roles. Suggestive of the poisonous atmosphere is a much-quoted exchange between Sarah and the leading (and older) dramatic actress Mme Favart. Catching Sarah in the theater grumbling "I'm fed up" and yawning, Favart snapped at her, "Mademoiselle, please remember you're not at the Odéon any longer." Sarah (curtsying to her senior): "No, madame—at the Odéon I would have said, 'I don't give a shit.'"

Her enemies were surely gratified at the reception of her first appearance in the theater, in November 1872. She had wanted to begin as Junie in *Britannicus*, but Perrin insisted she take the leading role in an old play by Dumas *père* called *Mademoiselle de Belle Isle*. She was distressed by the choice of play, shaking with stage fright, and undone by seeing her mother suddenly leave the theater a few minutes into the first act. Mme Guérard rushed off in a cab to discover what had happened, and got back to the theater only for the fifth act with news that Youle had taken ill but had recovered—just in time for Sarah to rally her forces for the final scenes. Sarcey, among others, reported his severe disappointment. Soon, though, she scored a real success as the unhappy Junie, betrothed to the noble Britannicus, pursued by the murderous Nero, and she was on her way, though not without setbacks, roadblocks, and the usual behind-the-scenes crises.

One of the key characteristics of the Comédie-Française was its emphasis on ensemble playing, and the principal actors all had their secure specialties and roles, the last major exception to this group approach having been Rachel, whose genius as a classical tragedienne immediately set her apart from everyone else, and who—like Sarah—would go her own way in defiance of tradition and convention.*

Sarah could charm the audience as, say, Chérubin in Beaumarchais' *Le Mariage de Figaro*, but given her temperament—her need to be the center of attention and in control—she couldn't for long fit into an ensemble: She was a star or she was nothing. Because of her beautiful voice and diction, the distinction of her poetry and the appeal of her person, she could win over the audience and the critics in secondary roles like Junie, or Aricie in *Phèdre*—in her memoirs she likes to point out that even in such lesser roles it was she who had the greatest success of the evening. But she hadn't yet been assigned the roles that would identify her as the company's leading actress.

Something that couldn't have been anticipated transpired to help her begin to achieve her dominance. A young actor known as Mounet-Sully (born Jean-Sully Mounet) had recently been taken on; he had been at the Odéon but in so minor a capacity that Sarah had hardly noticed him. Now she noticed him—and he her. Their partnership, on stage and off, would fascinate the public and win them immense acclaim.

Mounet-Sully was an imposingly big and ravishingly good-looking young man with tempestuous emotions, passionate in his work and in his life. A force of nature. There was no one like him on the Paris stage and, from his first days at the Français, his impact was overwhelming. He would never be an actor of great subtlety (one critic compared him to a tenor), and he could never be one of Sarah's tame "leading men," like a Pierre Berton; he was as big a star, as powerful a presence, as

---

*Again like Sarah, Rachel flaunted rather than hid her sensational love affairs and her pursuit of money—she, too, was criticized for her "Jewish" rapacity. Rachel, however, was somewhat protected by the nobility, the grandeur, of her acting; she was a supreme model of classicism. Sarah, in these early years, was seen as pushy and "modern"—fair game for caricature and resentment.

she was—his Oedipus as famous as her Phèdre, his Hernani as brilliant as her Doña Sol, his Hamlet the most admired of his time . . . until hers. And, again like Sarah, he went on forever, the leading man at the Français from 1870 to 1910. It could be said that their electrifying partnership restored the health of the company.

The repertory they worked in was hardly restricted to the classics. A steady diet of new dramas and comedies was always being served up, and by now Sarah was appearing in some of them. And whereas she had no serious rival in tragedy, there were other actresses of talent and appeal in contemporary works, the most popular of whom was the slightly younger Sophie Croizette, Sarah's friend from the early days, and a very different kind of actress and woman. Even physically they were of opposite types—Sarah, tiny, skinny, intense; Croizette tall, big-bosomed, a perpetually smiling countenance. (As Henry James, working as a theater critic in Paris, delicately put it, the "amplitude of her person has reached a point at which, in the parts of young girls, illusion tends to vanish.")

They were cast together in Feuillet's *Le Sphinx*, which gave Croizette a violent death-by-poison scene, of which she made a great deal—to some eyes, a great deal too much. Since death scenes were to become Sarah's stock in trade, it seems odd that she wasn't handed this one. Yet though she had the quieter role—the noble, betrayed wife rather than the tempestuous mistress—she exercised her muted lyricism to great effect, and felt that she had conquered.

All had not gone smoothly during rehearsals. There was a comical flare-up when, at the climactic moment of the play, which took place in a garden at night, a spotlight representing the moon was shone on Croizette, not on Sarah, who was approaching her across a little footbridge. Not surprisingly, Sarah balked. Perrin, Croizette's lover (which explains a good deal), who was directing the play, refused to illuminate her, on the grounds that Sophie's was the central role. Sarah respond-

Sophie Croizette

ed with an irrefutable argument. "Excuse me, M. Perrin," she cried, "you have no right to take my moon away. The stage directions specify, 'Berthe advances, pale in the moonlight, convulsed with emotion.' I *am* pale, I *am* convulsed, *I want my moon!*" When this got her nowhere, she walked out, and for two days it was unclear who would be playing Berthe at the premiere. At last, as opening night neared, it was agreed that *both* ladies would have spotlights, and harmony was restored. Fortunately, tensions of this kind never really ruffled the amicable relationship that had always existed between the two actresses.

These are the rehearsals that Feuillet described so charmingly to his wife, but in a subsequent letter, which I've never seen quoted, he paints a different and more worrisome picture:

> Yesterday I witnessed a very sad scene. Sarah was coughing from the very start of the rehearsal. I found her so much paler and more ghostlike than ever that I even suggested

we stop, but she insisted on continuing. Suddenly she
fell violently onto a sofa, stiff as a board, and crying out,
"I'm suffocating!" Pandemonium and confusion.
Everyone ran to her. She was gripped by a dreadful and
interminable fit of coughing—dry, fierce, interrupted by
frightful splotches of blood that stained her handkerchief
and her lips. Lying on the sofa, bent in two, she went
on coughing without a moment's break, choking, unable
to catch her breath. I can't describe the strange quality
of that scene: the theater in chaos, the semidarkness,
this elegant young woman with her lovely hair, the fine
perfume of her handkerchief and then the crimson
spots, the charming pale face stained with blood. This
real-life drama bursting out on top of the other, and
death setting its mask on the actress's pretty face—it
was extraordinary and appalling.

Immediately after *Le Sphinx*, Sarah—depleted and obviously ill—begged Perrin for a month's holiday, but he refused,
insisting, despite her doctor's protestations, that she rehearse
and perform a major new role during the heat of the summer.
The play: Voltaire's *Zaïre*, about which Provost had warned her
at the Conservatoire. Incensed at Perrin's obstinacy, and exhib-
iting what she recognized were bitter and childish sentiments,
she worked like a madwoman and on August 6, "in tropical
heat," took the stage. "I was determined to faint, determined
to vomit blood, determined to die, in order to enrage Perrin.
I gave myself entirely up to it. I had sobbed, I had loved, I had
suffered, and I had been stabbed. . . . Dying on my Oriental
divan, I had meant to die in reality, and was convinced that I
was in my death agony." To her amazement, when the curtain
fell she was not only restored but filled with energy. "I learned
that my vital forces were at the service of my mind. . . . I found
myself in perfect equilibrium, having given out everything of
which I was capable—and more. Then I saw the possibility of
the longed-for future."

The company hadn't performed *Zaïre* in twenty years, but now she and Mounet-Sully kept it alive for thirty performances, the longest run it had ever enjoyed. No wonder: Sarcey had written, "It was ravishing. It will be a long time before we see two artists play *Zaïre* with such perfect sympathy, two artists who bring such youth, such fire, such—dare I say it—such genius to their roles."

And then came the supreme test of Sarah's art—the turning point in her relation to the company and to the world: her first performance of *Phèdre*. Racine's great tragedy is the equivalent in the French theater to *Hamlet* in ours—a huge, exhausting role for the central character, requiring not only supreme talent but supreme vocal and physical stamina. Toward the end of 1874 Perrin summoned Sarah to his office and handed her the role—on four days' notice. (An older actress had declined to play.) Of course she knew much of the part from her studies and from having played the ingénue, Aricie, the year before, but this was a terrifying prospect.

Wisely, she went to her former teacher Régnier, the leading pedagogue of the theater, for advice and support, and he gave her the key: Seek sympathy for Phèdre the tormented woman rather than awe for Phèdre the implacable queen. In other words, be Bernhardt, not Rachel.

With Mounet as her stepson, Hippolyte—the horrified object of her incestuous passion—she took the stage on the night of December 21, suffering from the fiercest stage fright of her life. The first act did not go well—as always when she was nervous, her voice was too high and her speech too quick. But she rallied, and from the second act on, she gripped the audience. There was intense controversy about her performance as compared with Rachel's, but there was no doubt that she had succeeded. And this was only a first attempt. Over the following decades her Phèdre grew and refined itself, becoming her most admired role and remaining her biggest test, the one role she never took lightly. In 1908 Lytton Strachey wrote of it:

To hear the words of Phèdre spoken from the mouth
of Bernhard[t], to watch, in the culminating horror
of crime and of remorse, of jealousy, of rage, of desire,
and of despair, all the dark forces of destiny crowd
down upon that great spirit, when the heavens and the
earth reject her, and Hell opens, and the terrific urn
of Minos thunders and crashes to the ground—that
indeed is to come close to immortality, to plunge
shuddering through infinite abysses, and to look, if
only for a moment, upon eternal light.

Just over a year after Phèdre, in *L'Étrangère* by Dumas *fils*,
Sarah played the ridiculous role of Mrs. Clarkson, an American woman, the daughter of a mulatto slave girl and a southern
planter. (Henry James reduces this to "My mother was pretty:
he remarked her; I was born of the remark," and goes on to call
L'Étrangère Dumas' worst play.) Croizette was the much put-
upon duchesse de Septmonts. Strangely enough, each actress
envied the other's role.

These agitations did not go unnoticed. In a dispatch from
"Our Own Correspondent," dated February 16, 1876, the *New
York Times* reported,

Although Paris is in the midst of one of the most heated
political campaigns known since 1848, the main event
of the week has been the appearance of a new drama by
Alexandre Dumas at the Comédie Française. . . . Some
months have elapsed since this piece was first announced,
and many weeks have passed away since the roles were
distributed and the parts given out to the different artists.
And during this period there have been a thousand
difficulties to overcome. It was not without a world of
trouble that the principal artists of the Français could be
brought to accept the roles assigned to them.

The rivalry between Sophie and Sarah was a healthy
one, and certainly good for the box office, as Bernhardtistes

and Croizettistes fiercely championed their favorites. The fact that both *Le Sphinx* and *L'Étrangère* were basically worthless was irrelevant.

Sarah had been back at the Français four years when she scored another great success in an unlikely role (and another dreadful play). *Rome Vaincue* was a melodrama set in ancient Rome—a Vestal Virgin betrays her vows of chastity and is condemned to being buried alive, but her blind old grandmother stabs her in the heart to spare her so dreadful a fate. To the astonishment of the management, Sarah insisted on playing not the sacrificial heroine but old Posthumia. To Sarcey "she was nature itself, served by a marvelous intelligence, by a soul on fire. . . . This woman acts with her heart and with her entrails. She is a wonderful artist, incomparable, a magnificent nonpareil—in a word, an actress of genius." (James endorsed Sarcey's judgment: "The manner in which [Bernhardt] renders the part is one more proof of her extraordinary intelligence and versatility. . . . How it is that, to simulate blindness, she contrives for half an hour at a time to show only the whites of her eyes, is her own affair; the effect is highly relished by the audience.")

In her remaining years at the Français, Sarah appeared in only five new roles, apart from one benefit performance as Desdemona, opposite Mounet, in the fifth act of *Othello*. She was a surprising success in the elusive role of Monime in Racine's *Mithridate*, and again a surprise in Molière's *Amphitryon*—light, adorable, irresistible. (Mounet, though, was not a success: He was thrilling, he was beautiful, but his raw intensity precluded humor.)

The two greatest triumphs of these years were in works by Victor Hugo. His most famous play, *Hernani* (we know it best as Verdi's *Ernani*), had been the emblem of the Romantic movement when in 1830 it was first performed at the Français—as much a cause as a work of art. Despite previous revivals, it had never had the success it now enjoyed. The role of Doña Sol gave Sarah a superb opportunity to display the purity of her verse and the elegance of her person, and Mounet was a towering figure of romantic masculinity. Together they were magnificent. Alphonse Daudet wrote, "Never has she been so touching. Never has she displayed with such marvelous artistry her rare gift for feeling profoundly and expressing her feelings with so personal a touch. Those verses which everyone knows, which the entire hall murmured in anticipation, suddenly took on, through the harmony of her diction, a thrilling, unexpected beauty."

Even more gratifying was the response from Hugo himself. They were no longer on their old intimate terms, but to prepare for Doña Sol she went to him repeatedly for advice about her character and the verse. After the first performance, he wrote to her, saying, "Madame, you were great and you were charming; you moved me, the old warrior himself, and there was a moment when, as the deeply moved and enchanted audience applauded you, I wept." And with the letter came a diamond pendant in the shape of a tear.

Hernani became the two young artists' most acclaimed joint appearance, playing on and on through the summer of the Universal Exposition, one of the essential attractions of the season—an unheard-of 116 performances in all. It confirmed Sarah's place as the undisputed star of the Comédie-Française. For the first time since Rachel, audiences were coming to the theater to see a specific actor, not the company itself: When Sarah didn't perform, box-office receipts slipped badly.

Building on this triumph, the company finally staged *Ruy Blas*, of course reuniting Sarah and Mounet. Its success was at least as great as that of *Hernani*, and they played it in repertory throughout the following year. But this was yet another revival. By this time it was more than three years since Sarah had created a new role; in fact, throughout her years with the company she appeared in only four new full-length plays: *Le Sphinx*, *La Fille de Roland* (overblown tacky patriotism, but a success in the wake of the defeat of 1870), *L'Étrangère*, and *Rome Vaincue*. Everything else was either a classic—Racine's *Phèdre* and *Andro-maque*, Voltaire's *Zaïre*—or a recent play in revival, like the two Hugo dramas. She was still, despite her constant struggle to take charge of her own life, dependent on Perrin's dictatorship. And despite her incontestable status as the company's major attraction, she had not yet been made a senior *sociétaire*. It was clear from her behavior both inside and outside the theater that she was increasingly disaffected.

Early in 1880, with the theater in need of repairs, Perrin decided to transfer the company to London for a season at the Gaiety Theatre. The financial terms for the actors were poor, yet he tried to limit the lucrative private performances the stars would certainly be offered in the drawing rooms of London's elite. The actors, led by Sarah—"Mademoiselle Révolte," Perrin called her—asserted their rights and carried the day. In addition, digging in her heels, Sarah refused to go at all unless she was immediately made a full *sociétaire* for the duration of the tour—it was primarily a matter of billing. Fine, her senior colleagues said—let her stay home. But the English management announced that without the appearance of Mounet-Sully, Coquelin, Croizette, and—especially—Sarah, they would cancel the engagement; according to Louis Verneuil, more than half their bookings had been made on the strength of her name, and it was absolutely essential that she appear on the first night. At this—unwilling to jeopardize the company's English season—Sarah withdrew her conditions and agreed to go on the old terms, at which the *sociétaires* immediately granted her and Croizette full membership in perpetuity. The London season was saved.

She arrived in England in a gale of publicity organized by the impresario Edward Jarrett, who was representing her. She was met at Folkstone by luminaries (including Oscar Wilde) before proceeding to a house rented for her in Belgravia's Chester Square, which Mme Guérard had gone ahead to secure and to furnish with all the opulence and comfort Sarah required.

Sarah and Mounet-Sully in *Hernani* (New York Public Library of Performing Arts at Lincoln Center)

On opening night at the Gaiety, playing the second act of *Phèdre*, she started off too high-pitched and at too fast a pace, but she pulled herself together and was received with raptures, "although when the curtain came down, Mounet-Sully caught me as I fainted and carried me to my dressing room."

For six weeks she dominated the season with her brilliant performances, her antics (like rushing to a famous animal supplier in Liverpool to supplement her already notorious private zoo—her three dogs, her parrot [Bizibouzon], and her monkey [Darwin]—with a cheetah, seven chameleons, and a wolf dog, since the pair of lion cubs she really wanted was unavailable), and her acceptance by London society. When she was invited to meet this or that lady or countess on social terms, she was confused: "No society woman in Paris would think of asking me to her house except as an artist, and I would never ask her to mine. I thought—there must be some mistake." (Nor were false impressions easy for her to correct: Not only in 1880 but all her life—after nine American tours and countless seasons in England—she was hopeless at speaking English, or any other foreign language.)

What made it all the more remarkable was that she in no way tried to hide her irregular status as an unmarried mother: Beloved Maurice, now fifteen, was with her, and arriving at an elegant reception she would make sure they were announced as "Mlle Sarah Bernhardt and her son." Nor did her private life in any way affect the warm reception she had from England's leading actors. Not only Ellen Terry, who was also an unwed mother, but Henry Irving, Herbert Beerbohm Tree, and Mrs. Patrick Campbell were extremely welcoming.*

Her indisputable triumph with the English was, unfortunately, at the expense of her colleagues. Croizette, in particular, failed to make an impression, surprising Sarcey and other leading French critics who had crossed the Channel to report on how the company was faring abroad. But Sophie was wholesome,

---

*Terry's verdict appears in her memoirs: "How wonderful [Sarah] looked in those days! She was as transparent as an azalea, only more so; like a cloud, only not so thick. Smoke from a burning paper describes her more nearly! She was hollow-eyed, thin, almost consumptive-looking. Her body was not the prison of her soul, but its shadow. On the stage she has always seemed to me more a symbol, an ideal, an epitome than a *woman*. . . . It is this extraordinary decorative and symbolic quality of Sarah's which makes her transcend all personal and individual feeling on the stage. No one plays a love scene better, but it is a *picture* of love that she gives, a strange orchidaceous picture rather than a suggestion of ordinary human passion as felt by ordinary human people. She is exotic—well, what else should she be? One does not, at any rate one should not, quarrel with an exquisite tropical flower and call it unnatural because it is not a buttercup or a cowslip."

uncomplicated, normal. Sarah was exotic—and erotic. When she was ill one day and had to miss a matinee performance of *L'Étrangère*—*Tartuffe* was substituted—droves of disappointed patrons turned in their tickets. As she reports almost gloatingly in her memoirs, "Out of the forty-three performances given by the Comédie-Française, the eighteen in which I took part took in an average of 13,350 francs each; while the twenty-five other performances took in an average of 10,000 francs."

Furious at the way all the fuss about her was being negatively reported in the Paris press, Sarah wrote an angry letter to *Le Figaro*, defending herself and in effect resigning from the company. She was prevailed upon to withdraw her threat, but the constant attacks and resentment she endured, combined with the extraordinary acclaim and box-office power she was commanding, no doubt encouraged her to contemplate the unthinkable: quitting the Comédie-Française yet again and striking out on her own. In fact, given the chronology of events, it seems almost certain that she had *already* been contemplating the unthinkable.

On her return to Paris she found herself a highly unpopular figure: The French press had done its work all too well. She was warned by Perrin not to make an appearance at the theater's welcome-home ceremony—there was a cabal working against her. In response she showed him several anonymous letters she had received, later quoting in her memoirs from one of them: "My poor skeleton, you will do well not to show your horrible Jewish nose at the opening ceremony the day after tomorrow. I'm afraid it would serve as a target for all the potatoes that are now being cooked specially for you in your kind city of Paris." And she declared that she was not only determined to appear on stage, but would appear by herself, not as one of a pair, like the other actors: "I felt I ought to face the ill-will and the cabal alone."

> The public was delighted to see its beloved artistes again. They advanced two by two, one on the right, the other on the left, carrying the palm and the crown to place on

the pedestal of Molière's bust. My turn came and I
advanced alone . . . with a will that was determined to
conquer. I went forward slowly toward the footlights,
but instead of bowing as my comrades had done, I stood
up erect and gazed with my two eyes into all the eyes
turned toward me. I had been warned of the battle and
didn't want to provoke it, but I wouldn't run away from it.
I waited a second and felt the thrill and the emotion that
ran through the house, and then, suddenly, stirred by
an impulse of generous goodwill, the whole house burst
into wild applause and shouts. The public, so loved by
me and so loving, was intoxicated with joy. That was
certainly one of the finest triumphs of my whole career.

Now Perrin cast her in a play and a role she found particularly trivial, *L'Aventurière*, by Émile Augier. And she was
again unwell. Warning Perrin that she had hardly any voice,
she pleaded with him to postpone the opening for a few days.
He refused. On the first night she was unprepared and unin-
spired, and gave a poor performance. Sarah: "I had played badly, looked ugly, and been in a bad temper." The reviews the
next morning hammered it home, and that was the breaking
point—or, more probably, the excuse she had been angling for.
Immediately she wrote to Perrin:

> You have compelled me to play when I was not ready.
> You have accorded me only eight rehearsals on the stage
> and the play has been rehearsed entirely only three
> times. I was very unwilling to appear before the public.
> You absolutely insisted. What I foresaw has happened.
> The result of the performance has surpassed my anticipa-
> tions. . . . It is my first rebuff at the Comédie-Française
> and it shall be my last. I warned you the day of the
> general rehearsal. You have gone too far. I keep my word.
> By the time you receive this letter I shall have left
> Paris. Will you kindly accept my immediate resignation
> and believe me, yours sincerely, Sarah Bernhardt

Taking no chances, she delivered copies of this letter to *Le Figaro* and *Le Gaulois* and put Perrin's copy in his mailbox at the theater, so that he first learned of her desertion from the newspapers. It was too late—she and her maid had fled Paris for Le Havre, leaving instructions that no one was to be told where she was. When the company sent a minion to her house, she was gone: No one, as she tells us, was home—no one except Maurice and his tutor, her steward, her maid's husband, her butler, the second lady's maid, and five dogs. We don't know where the cheetah was.

The die was cast, and it was Sarah who had cast it.

The events of the next weeks make it clear that she had not merely been contemplating her departure from the company but had been planning it. Some time before the English season, she had been approached by the impresario Edward Jarrett about an American tour. She insists that she emphatically rejected the idea, but now that she was free to do as she pleased, she decided to go. However, there was time to kill before her New York opening in October. She had quit the Français on April 18, 1880, and just five weeks later she was back in London with a company she claimed to have rounded up overnight—and a new repertory of three plays, two of which she would play for years throughout the world, and neither of which was remotely classical.

Adrienne Lecouvreur, by Scribe and Legouvé, was the melodramatic story of the famous eighteenth-century actress who was murdered (with a poisoned bouquet) by her rival in love, the Princesse de Bouillon. It was a role written for and associated with Rachel, and it provided Sarah with one of her most moving death scenes. Sarcey, who came over to London to see it, wired home, "Never has an audience been so moved." Auguste Vitu, usually one of her harshest critics, wrote, "No one can doubt my admiration when I declare that Sarah Bernhardt, in the fifth act, rose to a dramatic power, a level of truth, that can never have been surpassed. . . . If the French public had heard—if it were ever to hear—her cry out with piercing tones, the way she did last night, 'I don't want to die, I don't want to die!' it would burst into sobs and ovations."

The other new role was in a hit play by Meilhac and Halévy called *Froufrou*—the nickname of a frivolous young wife who foolishly, carelessly betrays her husband and, in an agony of repentance, begs his forgiveness and dies at his feet. (Charm, superb clothes, and an anguished death by poison.) London, of course, had seen her die in both *Phèdre* and *Hernani* only a few weeks earlier, and on her first American tour she would die in six of her eight vehicles.

The weeks she played in England were triumphant, further proof to her that she was in no way dependent on the Français. (It sent representatives to woo her back, tactlessly suggesting that America would destroy her and offering to welcome her home from the American tour with a new staging of *Froufrou*.) During the summer she took her new repertory with her new company first to Brussels and Copenhagen (the Danish king presented her with the diamond-studded Order of Merit and had the royal steamer convey her to Elsinore), then on a whirlwind tour of twenty-five French cities in twenty-eight days. Her old friend Duquesnel, long since having forgiven her betrayal in quitting the Odéon, helped her throw the tour together.

During this period of frantic activity and superhumanly hard work, her health, always delicate, noticeably improved. And she understood why. "After this first taste of freedom I felt surer of life than ever before. Although my constitution was very weak, the ability to do as I wanted without interference and out of anyone's control calmed my nerves, and with a strengthened nervous system, my health, which had been undermined by perpetual irritations and excessive work, restored itself." She was sleeping better and eating better than she ever had before. She was riding high.

Finally, on October 15, 1880, she sailed for New York, regretting only that she had to leave Maurice behind. The advance publicity was enormous, and America was keyed up to receive her—she was both an irresistible artistic attraction and a focus of notoriety before she set foot in the new world. Henry James had grasped what was about to happen. Writing about the Comédie-Française season in London, he had observed her progress there with his usual acuity:

> It would require some ingenuity to give an idea of
> the intensity, the ecstasy, the insanity as some people
> would say, of curiosity and enthusiasm provoked by
> Mlle. Bernhardt. . . . She is a child of her age—of her
> moment—and she has known how to profit by the
> idiosyncrasies of the time. The trade of a celebrity, pure
> and simple, had been invented, I think, before she came
> to London; if it had not been, it is certain she would
> have discovered it. She has in a supreme degree what
> the French call the génie de la réclame—the advertising
> genius; she may, indeed, be called the muse of the
> newspaper. . . . I strongly suspect that she will find a
> triumphant career in the Western world. She is too
> American not to succeed in America. The people who
> have brought to the highest development the arts
> and graces of publicity will recognize a kindred spirit
> in a figure so admirably adapted for conspicuity.

XIII

WHAT HAD happened during Sarah's nine years at the Comédie-Française to raise her notoriety to such a high level? Her acting, of course, since there was now no questioning her professional ascendancy, which had come about through rigorous, almost obsessive hard work applied to a unique combination of gifts. But the events that had made her a byword throughout Paris—and, increasingly, overseas—had to do with her life off stage: her highly publicized extracurricular activities.

Her defiance of convention both inside the theater and away from it was a source of endless fascination to the general public. To begin with, there were her looks. She was still, in her mid-thirties, considered to be amazingly thin. She dressed not in accordance with fashion but according to her own idea of how to present herself to the world—she *made* fashion. Over the years she patronized the leading designers, most frequently Jacques Doucet, but they dressed her the way she chose to be dressed. (Not everyone wanted a hat crowned by a stuffed bat.) Her jewels and accessories came from the leading purveyors of such luxuries—Lalique, for instance. (She didn't like dark, somber jewels—"Jewels have to be gay," she pronounced.) And then there was Alphonse Mucha, the Czech designer she discovered who created her famous art nouveau posters as well as many of her costumes and ornaments, and who wrote in his memoir of her:

> Sarah's outfits were marked by their originality. She didn't
> worry about fashion, she dressed in accordance with
> her own taste; her tailors and couturiers, bogged down
> in their routines, were often thrown off balance by her
> demands. . . . Her dresses always followed the svelte
> shape of her body. She never had the bad taste to disturb
> the elegant cut of her clothes by a horizontal belt at
> her waist. . . . She countenanced only belts that dipped
> below her hips and had all kinds of jewels and always
> something tinkling hanging from them, echoing all the
> things that hung from her throat: collars, pearls, stones,
> chains, little charms of great beauty and great value. . . .
> One can say that rarely has someone's soul been more
> faithfully exteriorized. Every trait of her visage and every
> fold of every dress was profoundly conditioned by her
> psychological needs.

Furs—from chinchilla to ocelot to beaver—brocades, cloth ornamented with precious jewels and metallic thread

Sarah in her famous bat hat

were her element. In other words, she never dressed like anyone else, and since she didn't behave like anyone else either, she fascinated her entire world.

Her private zoo had been notorious well before she added to it so dramatically on her English trip. But far more notorious was the coffin that she kept in her bedroom. There are various stories (of course) about how she acquired it, but there is no doubt that it existed, that she carried it with her on her tours, and that it was meaningful to her. (Frequently, morbidly, she insisted that she wanted to die; fortunately, her extraordinary life force kept her safely alive.) Did she actually sleep in it? At one tragic moment in her life she definitely did. In late 1873 Régine was back living with her, painfully succumbing to tuberculosis after a short life of frantic social and sexual intemperance which her fragile physical system couldn't sustain.

To make her terrible bouts of fever and coughing more bearable, she was installed in Sarah's big bamboo bed, with Sarah sleeping next to her in her coffin on the floor so that she could tend her through the nights. The room wasn't large enough to accommodate a second bed.

"Three days after this new arrangement began, my manicurist came into the room to do my nails and my sister asked her to enter quietly because I was still sleeping. The woman turned her head, assuming that I was asleep in the armchair. Then, seeing me in my coffin, she rushed away, shrieking wildly. From that moment on, all Paris knew that I slept in my coffin." Immediately Sarah called in a photographer, arranged herself in the coffin with her hands crossed and flowers at her breast, and closed her eyes. The resulting image—one of the most famous in the vast Bernhardt iconography—was widely distributed, making a considerable amount of money for the photographer, and for Sarah. (And is there any reason to accept as true Sarah's amusing but less than likely account of all this?)

Régine was nineteen when she died, after a miserable life of neglect and prostitution. Sarah was devastated, falling so ill that her doctor insisted she go away to recover; even Perrin acknowledged that she was in need of prolonged rest and allowed her to go. But the sad death of her young sister led to further malice. Marie Colombier: "The funeral was superb, and Phèdre was drowned in tears. Old Perrin, seeing her weep so hard that her veil was in danger of going limp, pronounced, 'She's magnificent!' No member of the Company had ever reached such heights of pathos as Sarah did as she stood at the gates of the Père-Lachaise cemetery receiving the condolences of le tout Paris. As one journalist put it, 'It isn't a funeral, it's an opening night.'" Colombier got at least one thing wrong: It wasn't until a year after Régine's death that Sarah first played Phèdre.

Another of her more publicized activities was her highly visible career as a sculptor. Early in 1874—bored at the theater, denied roles she felt should be hers—she rented a large studio

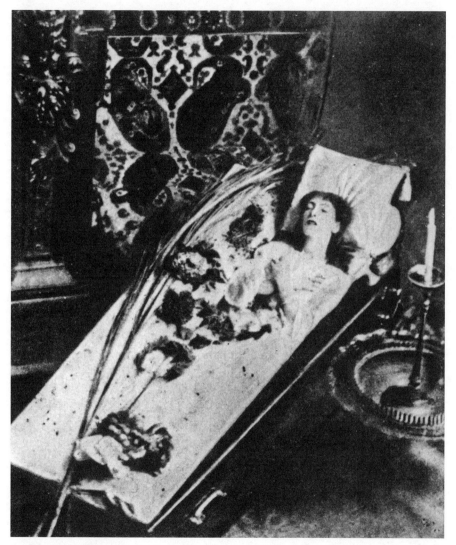

Sarah in her coffin

Sarah in her daring sculptress outfit

on the Boulevard de Clichy in Montmartre (it would one day be Picasso's) and set up as an artist. First, though, she ordered the perfect bohemian artist's costume: a white silk pants suit. Pants! After her daily morning ride in the Bois (her only exercise), she spent endless hours in the studio, receiving a crowd of friends and acquaintances at tea time. Her work paid off. For almost twenty-five years she exhibited at the annual Salon, even being awarded an honorable mention for her large group study *Après la tempête*, showing an old Breton peasant woman grieving over the corpse of her drowned son. Rodin pooh-poohed her efforts as "old-fashioned garbage," but they were taken seriously by others, and she pursued this avocation aggressively, holding exhibitions wherever she could—as she did on the first triumphant English tour. Gladstone, among twelve hundred others, attended the opening (they talked about *Phèdre*), and almost everything was sold. (She also painted, badly, and played the piano, ever more badly.)

Sarah's admired sculpture *Après la tempête*

Not only did her sculpting both attract yet more public-ity to her and supplement her income, it had the additional deli-cious benefit of enraging Perrin, who resented her attention to anything outside his theater. The fuss became so intense that her friend Émile Zola came to her defense in a letter to *Le Vol-taire*, asking why the press attacked her for sculpting, for paint-ing, for writing. "Not content with accusing of her being too thin, or of being mad, they want to censor her daily activities."

During the seventies, she had many close friendships within the artist community, most publicly with the very suc-cessful Georges Clairin, a handsome and charming portraitist whose large-scale painting of her coiled in white satin on a red divan, a wolfhound at her feet, is perhaps the most famous of the scores—hundreds?—of portraits made of her. Her liaison with Clairin was a happy one, and in due course it turned into a lifelong friendship: He became part of her most intimate circle and remained so until his death, in 1919.

Equally close to her was another talented artist, Lou-ise Abbéma, a mannish, monkeylike little woman who was a prominent member of Paris's lesbian world. Needless to say, it was rumored that they, too, were lovers—Sarah's supposed Sapphism was a feature of several of the romans à clef writ-ten about her. She may well have been bisexual, or perhaps she just liked giving pleasure to her friends and had no reservations about how to do it. Certainly, she and Abbéma made portraits of each other and posed together in provocative photographs, and of course she reveled in playing male roles. Whatever the truth about the sexual feeling or experience between them, Abbéma, like Clairin, remained an intimate friend until the very end.

From a professional point of view, the most important of her relationships with an artist was with the earthy (and sexy) Gustave Doré, the famous illustrator of Dante, Cervantes, and Poe, with whom she had an idyllic affair until it too faded into friendship. Doré gave her some tips about sculpting, and the two of them produced statues for the new casino in Monte Carlo designed by Charles Garnier, he of Paris's magnificent new opera house. Sarah's contribution was called *Le Chant*, a winged figure holding a lyre.

How good a sculptor was she? Her work has a quasi-professional if somewhat crude and sentimental look, at its most convincing in her busts of friends and colleagues like her pet playwrights Sardou and Rostand. Given her protean energy and her determination, she unquestionably pushed whatever ability she had as far as it could go. Even so, there were doubters. One close observer suggests in a gossipy and anonymously published memoir that while Sarah and her subjects and friends were away from her studio, other, more professional hands took over and did the serious work.

One of the most notorious episodes of her Comédie-Française years was her ascent in a hot-air balloon during the summer of the Universal Exhibition of 1878, when she was appearing to thrilled audiences as Doña Sol in *Hernani*. Tethered ascents in the balloon were all the rage, but Sarah decided to go up in an untethered one. A date was fixed, an orange balloon christened the *Doña Sol* was prepared to receive her, and on the appointed day, with word of her adventure beginning to leak to the public, she clambered aboard in the company of Georges Clairin and a young pilot.

The balloon took off, and after a while began to drift away from Paris, making slow progress. "At twenty minutes to seven we were about 2,500 yards above the earth, and hunger began to make itself felt." Luckily, their picnic was copious—foie gras, bread, oranges—and "the cork of our champagne bottle flew up into the clouds with a pretty, soft noise." But it got dark, it got cold, they didn't know where they were, and it grew clear that they had to land. Eventually they made it back to earth in a deluge of rain, and it was a long, uncomfortable time before the surprised locals could escort her to a train station, and a much longer time before, in the middle of the

Louise Abbéma

night, she was safely home, where a crowd of anxious friends had gathered for news of her.

This escapade had two immediate consequences, apart from the excitement in the press. Perrin—you can begin to feel sorry for him—had been strolling on the Pont des Saints-Pères with a friend, who suddenly said to him, "Look up in the sky! There goes your star!" Perrin, Sarah tells us with relish ("Putting Perrin into a rage was one of my joys!"), turned purple and "clenching his teeth, muttered 'She'll pay for this.'" He tried to get her to do just that, summoning her to his office and announcing that she was being fined a thousand francs for leaving Paris without permission. Taunting him, she told him that she would do as she pleased outside the theater, and that she would certainly pay no fine. "And besides, you bore me to death! I will

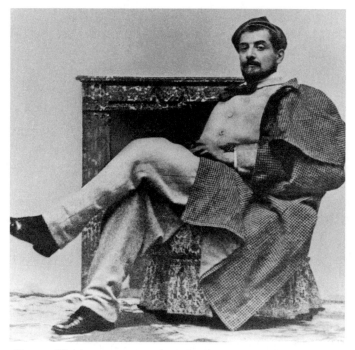

Georges Clairin

resign!" The next day she indeed sent in her resignation, but was persuaded by the minister of fine arts to take it back—Perrin, he acknowledged, had gone too far. The fine was remitted, and she graciously agreed to stay on. The reality was that she was such a big box-office draw that the theater couldn't afford to lose her.

Soon she had an even more impressive triumph. A book she dashed off called *In the Clouds: A Chair's Impressions, as Told to Sarah Bernhardt,* with delightful drawings by Clairin, was an instant best-seller, and deserved to be. Apart from its highly original premise—it was narrated by a cheap straw chair that had been placed in the balloon for her comfort—its jaunty style proved her to be a lively, amusing writer, a judgment that would be confirmed decades later when, in 1907, she produced her memoirs. Everyone was delighted with her balloon book except

Perrin—and Gustave Flaubert. He and Sarah had the same publisher, who he had hoped would be issuing an illustrated edition of his *Saint-Julien l'Hospitalier* for Christmas. Tactlessly, the publisher brought out *In the Clouds* in its place.

But the greatest source of notoriety at this point in Sarah's history was her love life, given the gossip and speculation it afforded the press and the general public. Clairin, Doré, Samuel Pozzi, who would become her doctor (Colette referred to him as "A sultan by his beard, a houri by his eyes"—he wasn't known as the Love Doctor for nothing), even the Prince of Wales—all were noted, but the main event was her tempestuous relationship with Mounet-Sully. ("You weren't this handsome at the Odéon, were you?" "I believe I was." "Ridiculous, I would have noticed!") Given their immense talent and striking looks, not only were they almost immediately paired on the stage, but soon they became a couple in real life. He was ardent, powerful, jealous, possessive, demanding—and he was a moralistic, highly conventional Protestant who believed in faithfulness, marriage, and monogamy. She was Sarah. Biographers Arthur Gold and Robert Fizdale in *The Divine Sarah* wickedly explicate the fatal disparity between them:

> Bergerac [where he was born] and the prudish advice of
> his God-fearing mother had hardly prepared Mounet
> for the casual promiscuity of women like Sarah. . . . His
> was a simpler world, where mothers were sacred, wives
> were submissive, and sweethearts were faithful. To give
> a woman the gift of his body was a release, an explosive
> proof of manliness, but to respect a woman who gave
> herself freely was unthinkable. His hope, he later revealed,
> was to raise Sarah from the mire of sin and lead her,
> good Calvinist that he was, onto the path of righteousness.
> Sarah had been to quite a different school.

Their letters, which Mounet carefully preserved in a silver box—including his to her, which he had demanded back from her—chart the turbulence of their relationship. For two

In the Clouds

Mounet-Sully

and a half years they grappled with each other—he, determined
to reclaim her, possess her, marry her; she, giving herself to
him, retreating, carrying on with her other lovers (including,
perhaps, the all-powerful Sarcey), as well as her regular group
of obliging benefactors—her *human* menagerie—who went on
chipping in to support her extravagant living arrangements.

Typical of her early effusions, Sarah to Mounet, January,
1873:

> Let me tell you that I love you madly, that I love you
> with all my soul, that my heart is yours. . . . It is thanks
> to you, my dear lord and master, that I no longer weep,

that I am filled with hope. To you, above all, I owe my knowledge of love, not the love I inspire in others but that love which I myself feel, which is mine to give. I am so happy to love at last, and to love you! . . . Open your being and let me enter it so that I am yours completely, and take, with this kiss made of memories and hope, all that is poetic and good in a woman's heart.

Typical of his:

Oh, Sarah! Sarah! My Sarah! You love me at last! It's true! It's really true! No, never again will I torment you with my jealousy, . . . I see you now, I know you, I possess you. You are we!! So fear nothing, you shall be happy. I shall place an aigrette on your brow, and cover your arms with lace made of kisses, since my naughty girl cannot do without luxury!!! Dear lover, dear friend, dear wife, dear beloved mistress, you too must have faith, confidence and hope. The future belongs to people of goodwill!! And we are young and strong, and we love one another!!

These were the early days. The next two years were a comedy of betrayals, remorse, scenes, anguish (his), impatience (hers), exclamation points (theirs). Meanwhile, their onstage partnership was an unparalleled success. (Jean Cocteau: "What could they possibly have to do with convention, tact, poise, these princes of the unconventional, these tigers grooming themselves and yawning before the entire world, these forces of artifice at odds with that force of nature, the audience?") Sarah was charmed by him, attracted by him, but his possessiveness maddened and repelled her. And in the long run, their goals were different. He was content to be the great male star of the greatest acting company in the world, which he went on being for forty years. She was determined to be the greatest and most popular actress in the world—and make a fortune being it.

Three of Sarah's distinguished lovers: Charles Haas ...

As the affair drew to its inevitable end, the tone of their correspondence changed.

Mounet, November 1874: "You have caused me great suffering, but I have loved you so! I forgive you for having deceived me because I sense that you're unhappy. I ask only one thing of you, that is to think that perhaps I was sometimes maladroit, but at least all my efforts were intended to make you a better person, to make you worthy of yourself. You did not want that. Perhaps it was beyond you. Be that as it may, I pardon you, and I pity *us*." And finally, in July of the following year: "I have suffered a great deal because of you, but I shall suffer no longer. I shall consider you dead until the day that prostitute's* body

---

*Mounet was hardly exaggerating. In the latest French biography of Sarah, Hélène Tierchant quotes police reports from the 1870s specifying the (highly respectable) customers—businessmen, members of Parliament—who "visited" her, what they paid her, the jewelry they gave her, etc. In other words, she was leading the life of her mother and aunt when she wasn't queening it over the French theater. Perrin wasn't paying the bills.

Jean Richepin, and   Gustave Doré

which resembles yours dies. . . . Come now, have the courage to accept the consequences of your evil fantasies, and try to behave as a gentleman would, since *nothing* could ever convince you to behave like a lady."

The most telling letter between them, however, stands apart from all the effusions. In early 1874 Sarah wrote, with extraordinary frankness, "You must realize that I am not made for happiness. It is not my fault that I am constantly in search of new sensations, new emotions. That is how I shall be until my life is worn away. I am just as unsatisfied the morning after as I am the night before. My heart demands more excitement than anyone can give it. My frail body is exhausted by the act of love. Never is it the love I dream of. . . . What can I do? You must not be angry at me. I'm an incomplete person."

For the proud and virile Mounet—years later he was to say, "Until I was sixty I thought it was a bone"—to be told that he hadn't been able to satisfy Sarah sexually was a near-mortal blow; she had hidden it well, experienced as she was in simulating passion. For Sarah, it was an acknowledgment of what was suspected and gossiped about by her circle: She couldn't achieve orgasm. Later, Marie Colombier would be explicit in *The Life of Sarah Barnum,* spitefully calling her "an untuned piano, an Achilles vulnerable everywhere except in the right place." Another witticism given wide currency: "She doesn't have a clitoris, she has a corn." In 1892 her lover/friend/surgeon Pozzi would remove her ovaries, and it was probably he who performed an operation that according to Edmond de Goncourt "allowed Sarah Bernhardt to achieve orgasm thanks to a surgical implantation gland that lubricated her formerly dry vulva." There are no secrets in the world of the theater.

Not all these specifics, of course, had made their way across the Atlantic, but reports of her genius, rumors of her extravagance, her morbidity, her cupidity, her sexual rapacity—and the fact, never disguised, of her illegitimate son—all contributed to the advance publicity that heralded the American venture. A dispatch from London to an American illustrated weekly well before she was to arrive gives the flavor of what she could expect: "Mlle Bernhardt is the unwed mother of four children. She does not veil her shame even under any pretension of marriage. She does not call herself *Madame.* Her bright boy, who accompanies her to the grand receptions given in her honor by the lords and ladies of England, addresses her as 'Mademoiselle, my Mamma.' It is a case of glaring, flagrant harlotry and bastardy, taken into the pure homes of English wives and daughters, and condoned by the men because she is so beautiful, so fascinating." No wonder she was the object of fanatical interest in New York long before she set foot there on October 27, 1880. Think of those four children! And all by different fathers—a hairdresser, a parricide heading for the guillotine, the Emperor Napoléon III, and Pope Pius IX!

XIV

THE VOYAGE was stormy, and Sarah went all out narrating it in her memoirs. Not only did she intervene to help a young woman in steerage give birth, but she saved the life of an elderly woman by grabbing her when a huge wave struck the ship and she was about to plunge headfirst down a dangerous staircase.

> "You might have been killed, madame," I said. "Yes," she answered, "but it was not God's will. Are you not Madame Hessler?" "No, madame," I answered, "my name is Sarah Bernhardt."
>
> She stepped back and drawing herself up, her face very pale and her brows knitted, said in a mournful voice that was scarcely audible: "I am the widow of President Lincoln." I, too, stepped back, and a thrill of anguish ran through me, for I had just done this unhappy woman the only service I ought not to have done her—I had saved her from death. Her husband had been assassinated by an actor, Booth, and it was an actress who had now prevented her from joining her beloved husband. I went back to my cabin and stayed there two days.

As it happens, Marie Colombier was a last-minute addition to the company (sister Jeanne had dropped out temporarily due to health problems), and she'd made an arrangement with a Paris newspaper to send frequent dispatches about the tour. (They were later published in the book *The Voyage of Sarah Bernhardt*.) At this time, Marie had not yet turned on Sarah, and although there's a sardonic tone to her reportage (Sarah is always "Dona Sol" or "La Grande Artiste"), and although she inflates her own importance, she's also a careful observer and, here, an apparently honest one. Her only mention of Mary Todd Lincoln: When they're disembarking in New York, "an elderly woman is trying to get past. A policeman holds her back to give way to Sarah Bernhardt. Someone informs me that this woman, called Mrs. Lincoln, is the widow of the president of the United States assassinated in the service of his country." So much for the plunge down the staircase.

But in her memoirs Sarah does not exaggerate the frenzied reception she received from the press in New York, orchestrated no doubt by Jarrett and his colleagues. After a determined interrogation by reporters greeting the ship, she's pursued to her hotel and after a quick nap is forced by Jarrett to receive the reporters' inane questions graciously. "What do you eat when you wake up in the morning?" (Jarrett quickly answers "Oatmeal," of which Sarah had never heard.) "What do you eat for lunch?" Jarrett: "Mussels." "What do you think of our overhead trains?" "Jewcatholicprotestantmahometanbuddhistatheistzoroastriantheistordeist?" "I am a Catholic, mademoiselle." Are you "a Roman Catholic or do you belong to the Orthodox church?" It was to be like this all across America.

She had decided to open her New York season with *Adrienne Lecouvreur*, a daring choice not only because this had been one of Rachel's most admired roles there a quarter of a century earlier, but because the character of Adrienne doesn't appear until the second act, causing anxiety and resentment in the audience, who were there only to see Sarah Bernhardt (and had paid premium prices to do so).

Even so, she triumphed; at her agonized death scene, she assures us, "there was quite an ovation, and everyone was deeply moved." On closing night, she played *La Dame aux camélias* (called *Camille* in America to disguise the fact that this was the infamous play about a courtesan), "and I counted seventeen calls after the third act and twenty-nine after the fifth." During this first New York run, she performed *Camille* and *Froufrou* six times each, *Hernani* five times, *Adrienne* and *Le Sphinx* three times, *Phèdre* twice. The success of *Camille*—which she had not yet played in Europe—was so great that by the time the tour was over, it had been scheduled approximately sixty times, more than one-third of her American performances.

The American response to Sarah took different forms. First, there were the critics, who on the whole were serious, contentious, and passionate. There was a considerable amount of comparison to Rachel (particularly in *Phèdre*, a number of the older writers preferring her grander, more austere and classical approach to Sarah's more womanly and emotional characterization). There was a good deal of complaint (deserved) about the quality of Sarah's supporting cast. This was essentially a pickup company, including the leading man, Angelo, about whom Sarah herself had few illusions: "He lacked nothing to be perfect but talent," she wrote in her memoirs, "but he had none and would never have any." (Presumably, his talent in bed was more convincing.) Rather than hire experienced—and expensive—actors, Sarah had put her money into her costumes and jewels, knowing that she had to make an impression of unprecedented splendor.

The critics had expected, on the one hand, an overpainted French seductress; on the other, a paragon of Comédie-Française classicism. Instead, they found a slender, elegant young woman with a ravishing voice and what seemed a revolutionary naturalism when compared with the strutting and bluster of the standard American acting of the period. Apart from *Phèdre*, Sarah was performing sophisticated French melodramas, usually with tragic endings. (Her death scenes came in for good-natured satirizing, as in a parodic advertising circular called "The Great French Dier." Among the "approved dies" on the list were "The Adrienne—A rich and lasting die of strong solid color shot with poison streaks" and "The Sphinx—A crawly sensational die. . . . Has fine green lights and foamy variations." Patricia Marks's scrupulously researched book *Sarah Bernhardt's First American Theatrical Tour* reveals a considerable range of reaction to her personal and professional life. Different cities had different responses to her acting. Boston embraced her, after a cautious beginning; straitlaced Chicago took against her at first, then eventually capitulated. Both New

Caricatures from Sarah's first American
tour, a) raining gold ...

Orleans and St. Louis admired her naturalness. But everywhere
her art was seen and judged in relation to her morals. American Puritanism was challenged most of all by the existence of
the illegitimate Maurice—proof positive that his mother was a
wicked woman, just like all those women she played. Poor frivolous Froufrou strays from her husband; "Camille," of course,
is a courtesan; Phèdre has an incestuous passion for her stepson; Adrienne is not only a mistress but an actress. But all these
at least had the tact to die in atonement for their sins, whereas
Sarah not only was alive but was raking in mountains of money.

Her supposed wickedness held an irresistible allure for
American audiences, who then found themselves moved by
her very human—her womanly—emotions. She was admired,

and b) as "The Modern Rizpah, Protecting her Son
from the Clerical Vultures"

condemned, glorified, emulated—and, in Montreal, actively
persecuted. In that intensely Catholic and deeply anti-Semitic
community she was the object of violent attack, and was actually threatened by riffraff both at the railroad station and at
her hotel. Yet audiences ignored the strictures of the Church
against attending her immoral performances over Christmas.
She may have been a "money-grubbing Jew," but she was also a
great French artist—and they could be proud. Once again, the
reviewers found her praiseworthy.

But whatever the reactions to her acting and her morals,
wherever she went she was first and foremost an Event, excitement about her arrival whipped up by an avalanche of publicity and accompanied by countless interviews, concocted anec-

dotes, and commercial capitalization. ("Bernhardt may come and go, but Neuralgine is the constant friend that will relieve your Neuralgia and Headache." Sarah: "I have had rare delight from the use of my Columbia Bicycle. It is matchless.") Stores

she shopped in cashed in on her name. Parodies of her acting proliferated—she actually attended a famous female impersonator performing as "Sarah Heartburn" in Philadelphia, and collapsed in approving laughter.

The humor magazines made her a nonstop target, much of the humor ugly—particularly a series of loathsome caricatures of her (supposedly) Jewish features and her (supposedly) Jewish greed for money—but some of it harmless and even witty:

Sadie!
Woman of vigorous aspirations and remarkable thinness!
I hail you. I, Walt Whitman, son of thunder, child
of the ages,
I hail you.
I am the boss poet, and I recognize in you an element
of bossiness
that approximates you to me.
Blast your impudence!—I like it.

And this draconian abridgment of *Camille* in the
Worcester Evening Gazette:

Act I
He—You are sick. I love you.
She—Don't. You can't afford it.

Act II—Paris
She—I think I love you. But good-bye; the Count is coming.
He—That man! Then I see you no more. But no!
An idea! Let us flee to the country.

Act III
His Father—You ruin my son! Leave him.
She—He loves me.
His Father—You are a good woman. I respect you. Leave.
She—I go.

Act IV—Paris
She—You again? I never loved you.
He—Fly with me or I die.
She—I love you; but good-bye now.

Act V—Paris
She—(very sick) Is it you? Is God so good?
He—Pardon me. My father sent me.
She—I pardon you. I love you. I die. (Dies. Tears,
Sensation, Curtain.)

In New York—unlike London—Society ignored her, except at the theater. But Commodore Cornelius Vanderbilt attended—alone and weeping—every one of her performances. And wherever she went she met the great and famous. She interrupted her train ride from New York to Boston to stop off in Menlo Park, New Jersey, for an encounter with Thomas Edison (he trotted out his new invention, the phonograph, and she obliged by recording a speech from *Phèdre*, sadly lost). In Boston, she paid a call on Longfellow (who refused to see her without a chaperone), hoping but failing to sculpt a bust of him. (A New York gossip column commented, "I'd give an old shoe to see the French sinuosity pottering about with her clay and chisels, while the silver-haired poet poses gracefully before her, reciting 'The Psalm of Life.'")

Her most distressing encounter was with a relentless promoter who in Boston inveigled her into coming down to the dry dock to climb onto the slippery back of a dead whale that he had preserved and was ballyhooing, then pursued her from city to city, presenting his whale as a fellow attraction and driving her wild with irritation.

Although she traveled in considerable comfort, with a private railroad car set aside for her, her maid, and Angelo, with her own cook in attendance, there were the discomforts of filthy hotels, dingy and inadequate theaters, and the unavoidable exhaustions of one-night stands. All in all, she appeared in about fifty venues, including such towns as Leavenworth, Kansas, and Titusville, Pennsylvania. The other actors, without benefit of private car or French cook, were miserable and bored—and their performances showed it. Marie Colombier in particular resented the lack of preferential treatment from her former best pal: "We live on preserves, sandwiches, biscuits, and sardines. Cold. Too late for dinner when we arrive at hotels. Sarah, needless to say, doesn't suffer at all. Other than the young male lead, no one approaches her."

Yet Sarah is intrepid under all circumstances. She exposes herself to real danger in scrambling over the ice floes at Niagara Falls. And she exposes the entire company to even greater danger as a weakened railroad bridge over a raging torrent crashes to its destruction moments after they cross over: They see it go down! (They've been rushing to make an engagement in New Orleans, and Sarah has bribed the engineer to take the risk of pressing forward despite the dire warnings of the authorities.) Sarah tells this story in a number of versions—three different rivers are named—but Marie Colombier's version, yet again, brings us down to earth. Once arrived in New Orleans she's shown a newspaper that reports the destruction of the bridge a good five minutes after they passed over it. No terror on board, no bribe, just a lucky escape. *Tant pis!* It's a good story.

Marie is more interested in informing the world that in New Orleans Sarah added an alligator to her menagerie—the cranky Ali-Gaga. It followed her everywhere—to the table, to the theater, to bed. (How, one wonders, did Angelo feel about *that?*) Alas, Ali-Gaga soon succumbed to a diet of milk and champagne. (Years later, in Paris, her pet boa swallowed some sofa cushions and had to be shot—by Sarah. It was clearly dangerous being one of Sarah's pets.)

The American tour lasted seven months, and when she boarded her ship for France, after a final successful fortnight in New York, she was tired but satisfied with her accomplishment—and rich. Henry Abbey, her hardheaded business manager, described her as "a business woman, on a business trip. . . . She came with an end in view—artistic repute and money." She returned to France with her reputation enhanced and her tour (she tells us) bringing in 2,667,600 francs. She had also tested her strength and endurance, faced the challenge of acting to multitudes who didn't understand the language she performed in, and learned not only that she could direct a company on the move while performing at a high level, but that she actually

Sarah touring America, (*above*) from the rear of her private Pullman car; (*opposite top*) in Colorado's Garden of the Gods; (*opposite bottom*) at Niagara Falls, seated fourth from right

thrived on travel. There would be eight more American tours, the final one during World War I, when she was seventy-three and playing on vaudeville stages.

Her memoirs, published twenty-eight years after the start of the first American tour, end with her return from it. (She never wrote a second volume.) Obviously, she saw this triumphant venture as a turning point in her life, and used the end of her book as an opportunity to look back and sum up:

> I conclude these memories of mine here, for this is really
> the first halting place in my life; the real evolution of
> my physical and moral being. I had run away from the
> Comédie-Française, from Paris, from France, from my
> family, and from my friends. I had thought of having
> a wild ride across mountains, seas, and space, and I came
> back in love with the vast horizon, but calmed by the

feeling of responsibility which for seven months had
been weighing on my shoulders. The terrible Jarrett, with
his implacable and cruel wisdom, had tamed my wild
nature by a constant appeal to my probity. In those few
months, my mind had matured and the brusqueness
of my will was softened. My life, which I thought at first
was to be so short, seemed now likely to be very, very
long, and that gave me a great mischievous delight
whenever I thought of the infernal displeasure of my
enemies. I resolved to live. I resolved to be the great
artist that I longed to be. And from the time of this
return I gave myself entirely up to my life.

In other words, at the age of thirty-five she had begun to
grow up.

XV

ONCE AGAIN, in her absence the French press and therefore the
public had turned against her—resentment at her defection
combined with malicious reports of her American adventure
(and financial success) had stirred up envy and anger. Luckily,
she was handed an immediate opportunity to redeem herself.
While crossing the Atlantic she had received a telegram plead-
ing with her to give a benefit performance in Le Havre, where
she was to land, in aid of the city's Lifeguard Society. She
rushed at the chance, and was greeted at the dock by a crowd
of thousands and a formal ovation ("You have now achieved in
two worlds an incontestable popularity and artistic celebrity,
and your marvelous talent, added to your personal charms, has
affirmed abroad that France is always the land of art and the
birthplace of elegance and beauty"). She chose to perform *La
Dame aux camélias*—no need to call it *Camille* any longer. It was
the first time she played it in France, and with her usual satis-

faction at her triumphs, "I affirm that those who were present at that performance experienced the quintessence of what my personal art can give."

There was still Paris and the theater world to confront. In her customary way, after three weeks of *La Dame* and *Froufrou* in London, she took the bull by the horns, managing to stun the audience at a gala performance at the Comédie-Française celebrating the tenth anniversary of the departure of the Prussian troops from the city in 1871. Without notifying anyone, she insinuated herself onto the stage in place of her old friend Mme Agar and began to recite "La Marseillaise" to orchestral accompaniment. She was dressed in white, a sash of red, white, and blue at her waist, and at the climax of her recitation she unfurled a large tricolor flag. When the audience first realized who she was, there was total disbelieving silence. When she finished, there was a tidal wave of weeping and cheering. She had recaptured Paris.

The restoration of her status was clinched by *Fédora*, the new play Victorien Sardou had waiting for her, the first of seven they would eventually do together. (*Théodora*, *La Tosca*, and *Cléopâtre* were among those to come.) It was—and they both knew it—a perfect vehicle for her, but she had committed herself to a six-month tour of Europe, so Sardou and his management would have to wait.

This tour was one of the high points of her professional life. Everywhere she went she was welcomed as the greatest of artists; as royalty. The crowned heads of Europe were at her feet (and very possibly in her bed). The king of Spain presented her with a diamond brooch, the emperor of Austria a cameo necklace, the king of Italy a precious Venetian fan. Archduke Friedrich, in Vienna, not only gave her an emerald necklace but insisted she stay in one of his palaces—"a queen doesn't stay in a hotel." When at a command performance at the Winter Palace in St. Petersburg she curtsied to the floor before Tsar Alexander III, he lifted her up, saying, "No, it is *we* who must bow to you."

The Russian excursion was stained by anti-Semitic dem-
onstrations in Kiev and Odessa. Fortunately, Sarah wasn't
aware of the dismissive remarks of the twenty-one-year-old
Anton Chekhov, still a medical student but writing satirical
sketches in a minor journal, who as an ardent Slavophile resented the hysterical adoration being offered to this ultra-French
celebrity: "She has none of the spark that alone is capable of
moving us to bitter tears or ecstasy. Every sigh Sarah sighs,
every tear she sheds, every antemortem convulsion she makes,
every bit of her acting is nothing more than an impeccably and
intelligently learned lesson." And again: "We watched Sarah
Bernhardt and derived indescribable pleasure from her hard
work. There were brief passages in her acting which moved us
almost to tears. But the tears failed to well up because all the en-
chantment is smothered in artifice."* Turgenev, too, found her
"false, cold, and affected" and despised her "repulsive Parisian
chic." She wasn't simple and true, like Russians. She was French!

None of the excitement, the adulation that followed her
everywhere meant as much to her as the appearance of the new
man in her life. Not Pierre Berton, her leading man on the
tour; not the young and handsome Philippe Garnier, another
of her leading men, with whom (of course) she had taken up;
but someone from outside the world of the theater. His name
was Aristides Damala, and he was a (genuine) Greek aristocrat

---

*In a short satirical sketch called "Sarah Bernhardt Comes to Town,"
Chekhov has a "Dr. Klopson" describing her performance to a "Dr. Ver-
fluchterschwein" solely in terms of her physical symptoms: 'Dear friend.
Last night I saw S. B. Her chest—paralytic and flat. Skeletal and muscular
structure—unsatisfactory. Neck—so long and thin that both the venae
jugulares and even the arteriae carotides are clearly visible. Her musculi-
sternocleido-mastodiei are barely noticeable. Sitting in second row orches-
tra I could detect clear signs of anemia. No cough. On stage she was all
wrapped up, which led me to deduce that she must be feverish. My diagno-
sis: anemia and atrophia musculorum. What is quite arresting is that her
lachrymal glands react to voluntary stimuli: Tears flowed from her eyes,
and her nose showed signs of hyperemia whenever she was called upon to
weep."

who was working in the Greek legation in Paris, a magnificent specimen of manhood with a romantic history as scandalous—and a ruthlessness as strong—as her own. "I'll be in St. Petersburg when you're there," he in essence told her. "I'll want to see you there." (He had been posted to Russia because the French government wanted him out of the country, his dissipations being too notorious to ignore.)

She was already in love, and in St. Petersburg she was overwhelmed with passion. At once Garnier was out of her bed and Damala was in it—on his terms, and when he chose to be. Although he had a decided Greek accent and no capacity for learning lines, Sarah decided that he was a born actor and put him on the stage (using the stage name Jacques), replacing Garnier in *Froufrou* and the faithful Angelo as Armand in *La Dame*. (Offended, Garnier quit the field.)

Even more extraordinary was her impetuous decision to marry Damala—she who had always asserted she would never marry. He doesn't seem to have been overeager for the treat, but that only spurred her determination. By now they were in the south of France, where there were legal and bureaucratic obstacles to their marrying—he a Greek Orthodox, she a Jewish Roman Catholic. Her solution was a frantic four-day dash to London, where they could be quickly and privately married in a Protestant church. (One of her telegrams to London friends: "What I have decided must be done, must be done, must be done . . . ") When she returned—late—for her engagement in France, she was Mme Jacques Damala, to the astonishment of the world and the outrage of Maurice, who detested this new stepfather, referring to him as "Monsieur Sarah Bernhardt." (Paris crowned him "La Damala des Camélias.")

This willful act was the greatest mistake of Sarah's life. Damala was a spendthrift, a gambler, an obsessive womanizer, and a bigot, and he didn't love her. Nor did he like being referred to as M. Bernhardt. (Greek aristocrats have their pride.) She persisted in her conviction that he was talented, but the

Jacques Damala with unknown actress. It's clear why he was not a favorite of the critics.

critics were less than kind. When she proposed that he play the male lead in the upcoming *Fédora*, Sardou drew the line; he was far too experienced a playwright to entrust his new venture—obviously destined for success—to a rank amateur. Damala was furious, and to kill two angry birds with one stone, Sarah took a lease on a theater, made Maurice its nominal manager (at eighteen, he was completely out of his depth), and put on a play for her husband to star in. It was a failure while, nearby, Sarah in *Fédora* was enjoying one of the great successes of her career. This did not help the marriage.

But nothing could have helped this marriage. Damala—ten years her junior—not only was unfaithful but flaunted his mistress in Sarah's face, taking off for Monte Carlo with the ingénue from his play and losing eighty thousand francs overnight at the tables. (Sarah paid.) He spent her money without compunction. He insulted her publicly—"That Jewess with the long nose . . . " He made scenes at her performances. And he fell deeper and deeper into serious morphine addiction. (Sarah's sister Jeanne appears to have been his supplier. Or perhaps he was hers.) Despite everything, Sarah persisted in trying to hold him, assuage him, support him.

Eventually, after countless indignities, her practicality reasserted itself and she threw Damala out, at which he went off to fight in Africa, then came back to further embarrass her. It wasn't long before his drug habit had done such damage that she took pity on him, rescued him, and saw him through his early death—in 1889, at the age of thirty-four. Not many of her circle mourned him. (Thérèse Berton, who had been on the Russia tour: "To me, Damala was the most cold-blooded, cynical, and worthless individual whom I had ever met. I could not bear the sight of him. His very touch revolted me." And Bram Stoker, in 1897, acknowledged that Damala was one of his models for Count Dracula.) Sarah had him buried in Greece, erected a monument to him there, wore mourning, and for some time persisted in referring to herself as Sarah Bernhardt-Damala, or the Widow Damala.

One of the great mysteries is why a flock of great women stars at the very summit of their art—assured in their talent, in firm charge of their careers, worshiped by both sexes—should have allowed themselves to be degraded by unworthy men: Isadora Duncan by Gordon Craig; Eleonora Duse by the vile D'Annunzio; Margot Fonteyn by her flagrantly unfaithful husband; Maria Callas by Onassis. In Damala, Sarah had found someone more domineering, more demanding, more ruthless than herself, and she gave herself to him unstintingly. Yes, the heart has its reasons, but in this case we can't help wondering what they were. Could it be as simple as his being the one man

Marie Colombier

who could do for her what Mounet couldn't: give her sexual satisfaction? She was to love other men, but although she was not
yet forty-five when Damala died, she never remarried.

The early Damala years were disastrous in a number
of ways. In 1883 her scourge, Marie Colombier, published
her infamous book *The Life of Sarah Barnum*, to which Sarah
foolishly reacted with public outrage. One of the great scandals of the day was provoked when Maurice invaded Marie's
apartment, challenging her lover and co-author to a duel (in
which he later prevailed), and was followed by Sarah, wield-
ing a whip and supported by her newest lover, the formidably
masculine poet and playwright Jean Richepin. ("Richepin is
even more fabulous than I am—that's why I love him.") According to whom you choose to believe, Sarah slashed Marie's
face before ripping the apartment to shreds, or merely chased
her out of the apartment before demolishing it. The scandal
not only galvanized Paris but made news in America. *The New*

The *Police Gazette*'s re-creation of Sarah's attack on Marie

York Times, December 19, 1883: "Mme Bernhardt in a Passion."
Subhead: "She horsewhips Mlle Colombier for publishing a
satirical book."

At this time also her beloved but unloving mother died,
"discovered one morning," Sarah told Lysiane, "lying on her
yellow sofa, dressed in a pretty negligee, with her head on a
laced pillow. Her beautiful hands held a small tray cloth which
she had been embroidering. She was smiling, a coquette even
in death. And I was so distraught that I fell ill." No doubt. Now
Youle's withheld love was eternally unattainable.

This death was soon followed by that of the drug-wracked Jeanne. Aunt Rosine had disappeared with some lover long before. Of Sarah's earliest ties, only faithful Mme Guérard remained. In addition, Sarah had dissipated huge amounts of money on the theater she had taken over to placate Damala and Maurice—a loss of some five hundred thousand francs—and, not for the only time, she had to auction off her jewels. Fortunately, although she loved acquiring things and did so almost compulsively, she never minded losing them. There was always a quick fortune to be made by trotting around the country, or Europe, or the world, with *La Dame*, *Froufrou*, and other sure things—like *Fédora*.

Because Sardou's play had been as great a triumph as she knew it would be. How could Sarah fail in the role of a Russian princess determined to revenge herself on a nihilist she believes has murdered her fiancé—only to learn that he's not a murderer at all, he's not even a nihilist, he's her innocent lover whom she's unwittingly condemned to exile in Siberia? The exoticism of the background, the agonies of passion and remorse, her endlessly protracted suicide-by-poison—this was the first of her great melodramas, expertly constructed by a master craftsman, opulently costumed and bejeweled, and giving her endless chances to thrill the audience. It made *Froufrou* and *Adrienne Lecouvreur* and *La Dame* look austere. To a large extent, *Fédora* set the pattern of her next two decades, although there would be excursions back into the classics as well as into a number of more literary or poetical ventures.

Jules Lemaître, one of Sarah's most acute critics as well as a close friend and lover, understood why *Fédora* was so perfect a vehicle for her:

> Mme Sarah Bernhardt, by her character, her allure, and
> her kind of beauty is eminently a Russian princess,
> unless she is a Byzantine empress or a begum of Muscat;
> feline and impassioned, gentle and violent, innocent

and perverse, neurotic, eccentric, enigmatic, woman-abyss, woman I know not what. Mme Sarah Bernhardt always seems like a very strange person returning from very far away; she gives me the feeling of the exotic, and I thank her for reminding me that the world is wide, that it cannot all be contained in the shadow of our steeple, and that man is a multiple being, diverse, and capable of everything. I like her for everything hidden that I feel to exist in her. She could enter a convent, discover the North Pole, have herself inoculated with rabies, assassinate an emperor, or marry a Negro king without astonishing me. She alone is more alive and more incomprehensible than a thousand other human creatures. Above all, she is as Slav as one can be; she is much more Slav than all the Slavs I have ever met.

XVI

NOW BEGAN a ceaseless succession of tours—mostly of tried and true repertory—interspersed with spells back in Paris to reestablish herself in the only place that really mattered, to triumph (or sometimes not) in new plays, and to enjoy the considerable fruits of her labors. There was a thirteen-month trek though the Americas, beginning in 1886. (In Argentina they granted her thirteen thousand acres of land—she never found out where—while Peru came up with a carload of guano.) There was a tour that lasted two and a half years—from early 1891 to fall 1893—that took in the Americas again, plus Europe and an extended triumph in Australia. According to Corille Fraser's *Come to Dazzle*, "The Australian press appears to have difficulty coming to terms with her Jewish side. It is constantly mentioned, and often immediately explained away by her being baptized or having attended a convent school." Fraser also tells us that in a book called *Great Events in Australia's History from Discovery to the Present Day*, Sarah's visit is listed as one of the great events of 1891—"along with the Queensland shearers' strike, the new Labour Electoral League winning thirty-six seats and the balance of power in New South Wales Parliament, the meeting of the First Federal Convention in Sydney and the first successful canning of apricots, peaches and apples in Hobart."

Most years, there were seasons in England; many years, swings through France. In late 1893 she took over the lease of the Théâtre de la Renaissance, which she ran as producer-director-star until 1899—except when she was on the road: Scandinavia, eastern Europe, and always America. Her energy was inexhaustible, her determination implacable, her fame unparalleled. There was practically nowhere she hadn't performed. One close friend recalled, "You could never mention any place, however outlandish, to which she had not been—thus, my mother once referring in conversation to the East African climate, she said, 'Oh, yes! I know Mombasa, I've played there.'"

Her touring was not just a matter of making money or of expanding her reputation. She loved it for its own sake; she loved being on the move. ("The cherished blood of Israel that runs in my veins impels me to travel. I love this life of adventure!") On the verge of leaving for the 1891–1893 tour: "I often take the train or steamer without even asking where I'm going. What does it matter to me? . . . I'm delighted to be off, and full of joy at getting back again. There's genuine and healthy excitement in moving from place to place and covering so much ground."

The bad years were behind her—the years of Damala, of scandal, of bereavements. These were the years of solidifying her personal repertory, apart from the perennial *Phèdre* and *La Dame*. Again and again she scored triumphs in Sardou vehicles. *Théodora*, in 1884, was even more sensational than *Fédora*: Sarah as the wicked Byzantine empress who betrays her husband, the Emperor Justinian, and, having poisoned her lover (she didn't mean to), calmly awaits her death-by-strangulation with a silken scarlet cord. (So what if the real Theodora died of cancer?)

❋ A Gallery of Roles ❋

LA DAME AUX CAMÉLIAS

LE PASSANT

RUY BLAS

L'ÉTRANGÈRE

PHÈDRE

ADRIENNE LECOUVREUR

FROUFROU

FÉDORA

THÉODORA

129

LA TOSCA

GISMONDA

CLÉOPÂTRE

Hamlet (photo Lafayette)

HAMLET

MACBETH

JEANNE D'ARC

L'AIGLON

Nothing was ever to surpass the sumptuousness of the sets or the magnificence of her costumes (in one scene, her biographer Joanna Richardson tells us, "Sarah wore a dress of sky-blue satin with a train four yards long, covered with embroidered peacocks with ruby eyes and feathers of emeralds and sapphires"). *Théodora* ran in Paris for a year. *La Tosca* in 1887 was as successful a play as it would later be as a Puccini opera: Her assassination of Scarpia thrilled decades of audiences. There was her gorgeous but claptrap *Cléopâtre* (1890). (In London, one dowager in the audience was reportedly overheard saying to another, "How unlike, how *very* unlike, the home life of our dear queen.")

And there was *Gismonda* (1894), a description of which, by Gold and Fizdale, gives a good idea of what Sardoodledom (in George Bernard Shaw's famous coinage) was like:

> A cruel fable set in twelfth-century Greece, *Gismonda* is the story of an Athenian princess who loves a commoner and, to everyone's surprise, succeeds in marrying him and living happily ever after. But not before the audience is terrorized by a heinous priest, an ax murder (committed by Bernhardt), a bloody massacre, and the grisly spectacle of a child being thrown to a ravenous tiger. Such heart-stopping moments were almost incidental to a production that offered impassioned speeches, the elaborately wrought splendors of a Byzantine church, processions of flower-clad maidens, and, as a finale, a wedding complete with pealing church bells, choral hosannas, and triumphal organ music. With all this, the show belonged to Bernhardt, an *art nouveau* vision in serpentine robes and a headdress of rare orchids.

Finally, there were *Spiritisme* (1897), scraping the bottom of the Sardou barrel, with Sarah as yet another unfaithful wife, this one pretending to be a ghost, and *La Sorcière* (1903), Sarah as a passionate gypsy burned alive at the stake during the Inquisition. Two years later, playing *La Sorcière* in Montreal, she would once again be the target of verbal and physical attacks encouraged by the current archbishop, who found this reproach to the Inquisition blasphemous: rotten eggs pelting the stage, stones and sticks pounding her carriage on the way to the railroad station, cries of "Kill the Jewess."

Yet even while Sarah was benefiting from her unprecedented collaboration with Sardou, she was trying other vehicles and other playwrights. In 1890 she gave Paris her first interpretation of Joan of Arc, every night stopping the show when, questioned at her trial about her age, she would step forward, face the audience, and calmly but firmly proclaim, "Nineteen." She was, as everyone knew, forty-six, and—recently, proudly— a grandmother. She pulled off the same *coup de théâtre* nearly twenty years later in another Joan of Arc vehicle—only now she was a great-grandmother.

In 1895 she first met Edmond Rostand, "my darling poet." He was only twenty-six, with one modest play at the Français behind him. Even so, she at once took on his poetical symbolist drama *La Princesse lointaine*, which cost her—and lost her—more than two hundred thousand francs. But as she said, "Too bad. If you're an artist, you can't not stage *La Princesse lointaine*." In any case, forty performances of *La Dame* quickly recouped her losses.

Were Sarah and Edmond ever lovers? If so, it was pro forma, and not for long; she was always close to his charming wife, Rosemonde, as well as to their son, Maurice. In 1897 Rostand went on to create what was probably the most successful play ever written for the Comédie-Française, *Cyrano de Bergerac*, for the greatest of France's comic actors, Coquelin. In the same year, Sarah produced Edmond's *La Samaritaine*, which the young playwright described to a journalist as the story of "a courtesan like Liane de Pougy who meets Christ, then returns to Paris to preach the Holy Gospel to her depraved friends." (Shades of *Thaïs!*) She played it during Holy Week for the next fifteen years.

And then in 1900 Rostand provided Sarah with *L'Aiglon*, the story of the duc de Reichstadt, Napoléon's dying exiled son. By this time, Sarah was a confirmed mistress (master?) of trouser roles, but these trousers belonged to a twenty-year-old. *L'Aiglon* premiered at a moment of renewed patriotic fervor in a France torn apart by the Dreyfus affair, and the play's Napoleonic connection roused audiences to a fever pitch of enthusiasm. At the opening night, "people were crying everywhere," wrote Maurice Baring; the play "was a progression of cunningly administered thrills, which were deliriously received by a quivering audience." Others reported (well-orchestrated) tumult and delirium, and curtain calls beyond number. Several commentators suggest that it was the most successful opening night in the history of the French stage. In the *L'Aiglon* iconography, Sarah has an unfortunate pouter-pigeon look, at least to our modern eyes; at fifty-six she was no longer slim. But back then, no one seemed to notice or care.

The year before *L'Aiglon*, Sarah had given up the Théâtre de la Renaissance and assumed management of the newly renamed Théâtre Sarah Bernhardt, with a seating capacity almost twice that of the Renaissance and with her name high on the façade spelled out in 5,700 light bulbs—electricity was the latest scientific sensation. (It was only in 1967—after an interruption during the German occupation—that it became the Théâtre de Ville, but the Café Sarah Bernhardt retains its name and is still thriving on its prominent corner of the Place du Châtelet, next door to her old theater.) *L'Aiglon* sold out the new theater for eight months and closed only because Sarah was taking it to America, with the added excitement of Coquelin playing an important but secondary role in exchange for Sarah agreeing to play Roxanne to his Cyrano. They had been great friends since the Conservatoire and loved working together. On this tour he was Scarpia to her Tosca, and frequently just before the third-act assassination scene, she would jump up backstage and shout, "Let's go kill Coq!" (He would also play Armand's father in *La Dame* and First Gravedigger to her Hamlet, while she played second fiddle to him in Molière's *Les Précieuses ridicules*.)

L'Aiglon is—let's face it—an overlong, overwritten patriotic verse drama. ("And all the arms! And all the arms I see! / The handless wrists! The hands with shattered fingers! / The monstrous harvest which a mighty wind / bends me-ward with a curse!") It went with her everywhere; she went on playing it even after her leg was amputated, when she was over seventy. And it went on exerting emotional power: On one of Sarah's numerous farewell American tours, for instance, little Mamie Doud (not yet Eisenhower) saw it in Denver and, according to her biographer, "was convulsed by heartbroken sobs" as the Eaglet expired in the arms of his last loyal aide. Its immense popularity is confirmed, as Gerda Taranow tells us in her essential book *Sarah Bernhardt: The Art within the Legend*, by the number of parodies it inspired. There were at least nine, as opposed to three or four for *Théodora* and four for *Cléopâtre*. (For *Hamlet*, only one.)

Not long before playing her late-adolescent duc de Reichstadt, she had assumed two far more distinguished male roles. In 1896 she produced Alfred de Musset's immense poetic drama *Lorenzaccio* of 1834, so daunting a prospect that it had never before been staged. (And she herself truncated it savagely.) One of her most severe critics wrote, "I have never seen anything equal to what she gave." And (her friend) Anatole France said:

> We know what a work of art this great actress can make
> of herself. Even so, in her latest transformation she is
> astonishing. She has formed her very substance into a
> melancholy youth, truthful and poetic. She has created a
> living masterpiece by her sureness of gesture, the tragic
> beauty of her pose and glance, the increased power in the
> timbre of her voice, and the suppleness and breadth of
> her diction—through her gifts, in the end, for mystery
> and terror.

Sarah with the great Coquelin

Lorenzaccio ran for only two months, but she had carried off an impossible task, lost a lot of money, and fulfilled a long-standing ambition.

Then, in 1899, came *Hamlet*, the most controversial of all her ventures. There had been Hamlets in France throughout the nineteenth century (Mounet-Sully's one of the most admired), and there had been numerous women Hamlets both in England and France. But the traditional French Hamlet, as Gerda Taranow explains in *The Bernhardt Hamlet*, her brilliant exegesis of Sarah in this role, was poetical, indecisive, a languishing figure from the Romantic period. That was not Sarah. First, she rejected the standard verse translation and commissioned a new prose version that preserved more of the text than any of the English or French *Hamlet*s of the day: Her produc-

Sarah with Réjane as Pierrot and Columbine

tion ran for more than four hours. Most important, she saw Hamlet as youthful, masculine, determined: From the moment he concludes that his father was indeed murdered by Claudius, his path is set, and it's only a matter of finding the right circumstance before he takes revenge. As she wrote in a letter to an anonymous English critic, "I am reproached for being too active, too virile. It appears that in England Hamlet must be played as a sad German professor. . . . There are those who are absolutely determined to see in Hamlet a woman's soul, weak and indecisive; but I see the soul of a resolute, sensible man." (As she remarked when challenged about playing so many men, "It's not that I prefer male roles, it's that I prefer male minds.")

Even before the first performance she was being attacked. As one French biographer put it, wasn't it enough for

Sarah with Mrs. Patrick Campbell as Maeterlinck's
Mélisande and Pelléas

her to obliterate all her female rivals, was she now going into competition with all the men as well? Lorenzaccio was bad enough, but Hamlet? What next: her Othello strangling Mounet-Sully's Desdemona?

Hamlet ignited passionate responses wherever she played it, and she played it everywhere and often. After its premiere she took it on tour to England and Europe while her new theater was being completely redecorated. When *Hamlet* returned to Paris, it was to a theater whose walls were covered in yellow velvet, a radical break from the traditional red. Sarah now had the professional home she would keep for the rest of her life, complete with a five-room suite near the stage where she dined and entertained and occasionally slept—she was a mistress of the catnap.

Critics everywhere were divided. For some, the role being taken by a woman was an obstacle they couldn't surmount. Most famous was Max Beerbohm's review, entitled "Hamlet, Princess of Denmark," which ended, "One felt that Hamlet, as portrayed by her, was, albeit neither melancholy nor a dreamer, at least a person of consequence and unmistakably 'thoro'bred.' Yes! the only compliment one can conscientiously pay her is that her Hamlet was, from first to last, *très grande dame*." Maurice Baring, on the other hand, believed it was the first time the role had ever been properly interpreted, and specifically noted that "whereas most Hamlets seem isolated from the rest of the players, as if they were reciting something to the audience, this Hamlet spoke to the other persons of the play, shared their life, their external life, however wide the spiritual gulf might be between them and Hamlet. This Hamlet was in Denmark, not in splendid isolation, on the boards, in order to show how well he could spout Shakespeare's monologues, or that he was an interesting fellow. . . . The whole performance was natural, easy, life-like, and princely." And Clement Scott, the conservative dean of London's theater critics (and author of a book called *Some Notable Hamlets*), praised her for "that rare vein of humour, that essential capriciousness which are in the very veins of Hamlet. . . . The whole thing was imaginative, electrical and poetical." Indeed, to Scott Sarah was "the greatest artist I have ever seen. As Hamlet I see her a greater artist than ever, because her task was heroic in its significance and importance."

The controversy pursued her to America, where William Dean Howells, as Taranow tells us, "dismissed her Hamlet as triple impertinence: not merely French and feminine, but Jewish as well." In response, the critic for the *New York Times* wrote, "I do not object to seeing a woman in a male role if she can act it. Sarah Bernhardt certainly can act Hamlet well enough to justify her attempt." He concluded that if Shakespeare "belongs to all the world, he belongs to the French; if to all ages, to the

present age! Surely, then, we ought to respect the French interpretation of him and, if it differs from ours, 'as a stranger, give
it welcome.'" But he had nothing to say on the Jewish question.

Taranow's book uses every possible scrap of evidence to
reveal exactly what Sarah did with the role—the closest reading of a stage performance I know, anatomizing all the original
subtleties of staging and gesture she brought to it. And her account provides further evidence of the extraordinary focus, intelligence, and labor Sarah brought to her work. (Nearly all the
testimony we have from her co-workers confirms her almost
rabid attention to detail, her constant rethinking of her roles,
and her insatiable energy—as ready to throw herself into sewing a costume as into changing a crucial entrance in *Phèdre* at
the last moment, after having played it for thirty years.)

Miraculously, we have a glimpse of her Hamlet on a
scrap of film—less than a minute and a half long, and available on YouTube—that captures the fatal duel with Laertes.
It was made as early as 1900, her first film appearance, shot
only a year after she first performed the role—and she's remarkably effective. Sarah was then fifty-six, and she not only
looks twenty years younger but can easily be taken for a male
. . . and a prince. She's somber, quick, natural—easily expert with
her sword and clearly used to dueling. There's nothing campy or
feminine about her; she's manly and she's coolly resolved. This
isn't an exhibition of virtuoso acting—it's modest, in fact. But
it's certainly a vindication of her right to perform the greatest of
male roles, and a welcome clue as to how she pulled it off.

In 1898, when she was preparing her Hamlet, she talked
about him with her journalist-biographer, Jules Huret: "I think
his character is a perfectly simple one. He is brought face to
face with a duty, and he is determined to carry it out. All his
philosophizing and temporary hesitation does not alter the basis of his character. His resolution swerves, but immediately returns to the channel he has marked out for it. I know this view
is heterodox, but I maintain it. It is just as well to have a decided

opinion of one's own, and adhere to it." From the very beginning of her life Sarah lived by those latter words, and perhaps her own unrelenting determination had something to do with her concept of a simple, determined Hamlet. If he wasn't really like that, he *should* have been.

During the late 1890s and the early years of the twentieth century, Sarah did dip her toe into the more naturalistic drama that was overtaking the theater—and that was seen as the province of Eleonora Duse. Her only brush with Ibsen was *The Lady from the Sea:* one performance, in Geneva, although she once mentioned to Jules Renard that she had dreamed of playing *A Doll's House* but finally found Ibsen too deliberate, too calculated. She toured in Sudermann's *Magda*, another Duse role, and did well with it. There was no Chekhov, no Strindberg. She kidnapped a D'Annunzio play from Duse, *La città morta*, but it was a disaster.

She was Judas, she was Werther, she was (Hugo's) Lucrezia Borgia, she was England's Queen Elizabeth, she was the Empress Josephine, she was Francesca da Rimini, she was Marie Antoinette, she was Madame X, she was St. Teresa (hardly a case of typecasting, one biographer remarks). She played a score of new roles in plays that made no impression then and no one has remembered since. In the affecting *Pauline Blanchard*, premiered in Buenos Aires, she played a peasant woman, but although she took it to Australia, even to London, she never brought it to Paris: As she said, her public there didn't want to see her as a peasant, being *tutoyered* by a lot of farmers; they wanted to see her in beautiful dresses.

Her impulses as she grew older were less toward the sanguinary and more toward the literary, the fanciful, the poetical. In 1904 she played Maeterlinck's Pelléas to Mrs. Patrick Campbell's Mélisande (in French, of course) in both Paris and England—something of a success, even if one ungrateful Irish critic said of these two formidable actresses, "They are both old enough to know better." Oscar Wilde wrote his *Salome* for her, again in French, but the English censors found it blasphemous and the project was shelved. And in 1920, when she was seventy-five and with only one leg, she finally played Racine's great drama *Athalie:* She could be discovered sitting on her throne or be carried onstage in a litter, the way queens of antiquity ought to be transported. It was one of the very few old-women roles she ever undertook. She scheduled three performances of *Athalie* but had so great a critical success that she ran it for three weeks. And soon after it closed she was back on stage in *Daniel,* successfully impersonating a thirty-year-old male drug addict.

XVII

FROM THE MOMENT she quit the Comédie-Française in 1880 until her death, forty-four years later, Bernhardt was in complete control of her career. There was no annoying Perrin to tell her what plays to appear in, and with whom, and for how long. There were no rivals, only male leads (whom she had chosen). Playwrights vied for her attention. Leading artists and composers were at her disposal—Massenet for *Théodora,* Gounod for *Jeanne d'Arc,* Saint-Saëns, d'Indy, Reynaldo Hahn. As we have seen, she was the favorite of the great couturiers, since she set fashions. Her tours were for the most part sensational successes. Step by step she had morphed from being a figure of scandal to being a magnificent artist to being venerated as a great symbol of, and ambassador for, France.

Perhaps the most decisive moment in her public progress to artistic glory—the event that set her even farther apart than she already had been from everyone else in her profession—was Sarah Bernhardt Day, a brilliantly organized event that took place on December 9, 1896. The high point was a banquet in her honor, sponsored by a large group of the leading figures of the day, including playwrights Sardou, the young

Sarah Bernhardt tribute day; program cover by Alphonse Mucha

Rostand, and Coppée, whose *Le Passant* had started her on her way almost thirty years earlier; writers like Jules Renard, Léon Daudet, Jules Lemaître, Catulle Mendès; fellow actors like Coquelin; artist friends like Clairin, Abbéma, and Alphonse Mucha. The president of France sent a representative. The minister of fine arts was seated beside Sarah at the luncheon (at the Grand Hôtel) for five hundred guests in full evening dress. One witness described her entrance down a winding staircase, in a white dress embroidered in gold and trimmed with sable: "Her long train followed her like a graceful tame serpent. At every turn she bent over the railing and twined her arms like an ivy wreath round the velvet pillars while she acknowledged the acclamations with her disengaged hand. Her lithe and slender body scarcely seemed to touch the earth. She was wafted toward us in a halo of glory."

Following "A Hymn to Sarah Bernhardt," everyone proceeded to her theater to watch her as the old blind woman in the fourth act of *Rome Vaincue* and in the first act of *Phèdre*. And finally the recitation of five newly composed sonnets by five leading poets, climaxed by Rostand's famous tribute to the *reine de l'attitude et princesse des gestes*—queen of the pose and princess of the gesture. (It sounds better in French.) "What a triumph for Rostand," said the sardonic Renard; "it's as if his sonnet was in five acts." Ovations, tears, embraces. The whole event was more than a celebration, it was a coronation. Maurice was weeping: "Nobody knows my mother—what a good, fine woman she is."

The relationship between Sarah and Maurice was as mutually adoring, as utterly agreeable as a mother-son relationship can be, short of psychopathology. They were so close in age—twenty years—that he might have been her younger brother if he weren't also, in his elegance and style, the kind of ideal husband that she fantasized his (presumed) father, the Prince de Ligne, might have been. From the start, she raised him to be an

Sarah and Maurice

aristocrat, showering on him every luxury and indulgence. "All I expect from Maurice," she's quoted as saying, "is to be well dressed." He was poised, handsome, elegant, a superb horseman, an expert swordsman (who frequently dueled to defend her honor), a serial adulterer, and an inveterate gambler, squandering fortunes at the gaming tables. (They were Sarah's fortunes, and she was always there to pay his debts.)

She was also (publicly) indulgent about his two marriages, particularly since the first was to the Polish Princess Marie-Thérèse Jablonowska, a pretty, accommodating girl known as Terka, who was willing to share her husband with his mother. They lived very close to Sarah's house in the rue Pereire and Maurice saw his mother daily—at her home and usually again at the theater. There were happy family dinners at Sarah's every Sunday, particularly happy once Maurice and Terka had

Sarah and Maurice

produced two daughters, Simone and Lysiane. To Sarah, family always came first, and—like Marlene Dietrich, another symbol of eternal and public youthfulness—she was thrilled to be a grandmother. (The entire family except Maurice, who called her "Maman," addressed her as "Great"—in English, a language she barely spoke.)

There are hints that Terka may have felt overwhelmed, even resentful of the relentless maternal presence. Reynaldo Hahn, in his charming memoir of Sarah, recalls being alone in a carriage with Terka: "We discuss Sarah and Maurice; melancholy reflections on mother and son by the wife." But what choice did she have? Not only did Maurice adore his mother, he lived off her. Hélène Tierchant's biography claims that Terka was so desperate over her husband's compulsive infidelities that she procured a legal separation and retired for

Sarah with her family. Standing, left to right: Saryta (Jeanne's daughter), Damala, Sarah; seated, Terka and Maurice Bernhardt

a while to England. In any case, by the time she died, in 1910, she was so in the shadow of her mother-in-law that, as one acerbic biographer put it, "You could barely notice her disappearance." Soon after her death, Maurice married a pretty young Parisienne.

Only once in the almost sixty years of their intimate contact with each other was there a breach between Sarah and her son, but it was a deep one. The event that shattered the unity of France, the Dreyfus affair, also shattered the family. Maurice—raised as a Catholic aristocrat, yet undoubtedly self-conscious about his off-key background (one-quarter Jewish, son of an actress, illegitimate)—was passionately devoted to the anti-Dreyfusard, pro-army cause: There was no doubt in his mind that the Jewish Captain Alfred Dreyfus was guilty of having passed military information to the Germans, and that he fully deserved his incarceration on Devil's Island.

But there was no doubt in Sarah's mind about Dreyfus's innocence—not that she was ever in doubt about anything. Although she was a sincere if hardly devout Catholic, there was never a question of her forgetting that she was also a Jew, even if the world would have let her forget it. For decades she had been hatefully caricatured, even persecuted (as in Canada and Russia and Germany) for her "Jewish" cupidity and coarseness. The virulent anti-Semitism that broke out during the Dreyfus affair inspired the most ugly vilifications (Jews were "pimps, chancres, thieves, synagogue lice"). In 1898 a notorious anti-Semitic book—*Les Femmes d'Israel*—proclaimed that "whether initiated into the worship of God by Gemara or by the catechism, Sarah Bernhardt is neither more nor less than a Jewess, and nothing but a Jewess."

A number of her distinguished Jewish friends and colleagues—Arthur Meyer, Catulle Mendès (son of a rabbi)—sided with the anti-Dreyfusards. Sarah, supported by others of her circle—Sardou, Rostand, Hahn, Clairin—fearlessly stood with the Dreyfus defenders, most famously rushing to side with her friend Zola when he wrote his impassioned "J'accuse." Headline from the right-wing press: "The great actress is with the Jews against the army." In other words, she was a traitor. To Sarah this was the supreme outrage. Her patriotism had always been unimpeachable, as she had demonstrated during the 1870 war. She may have had Dutch and/or German blood, she may have proudly proclaimed "I am a daughter of the great Jewish race," but she also felt herself French to the core.*

At the first crisis of the affair, the 1894 trial at which Dreyfus was found guilty of treason, the family situation became untenable, friendly relations between mother and son impossible. "I no longer know you," Sarah shouted at Maurice, flinging her napkin to the floor at one of the inevitable Sunday family lunches. Maurice grew so angry that he not only ceased speaking to his mother but, with Terka and their first daughter, Simone, retreated to Monte Carlo. For a year he remained completely cut off from his mother—the only time in his life that he behaved independently. Of course the domestic situation eventually repaired itself, but almost a dozen years later, in

---

*Sarah's experience of her Jewish/Gentile identity oddly parallels that of Benjamin Disraeli, born forty years before her. At the insistence of her father, Sarah was officially converted to Catholicism just before her twelfth birthday, while Disraeli's secular father, Isaac, had Benjamin baptized into the Church of England just before he turned thirteen—that is, before he was to be bar mitzvahed and could make the choice for himself. In both cases, their younger siblings were converted at the same time they were. Both the star and the future prime minister not only always considered themselves Jewish but asserted their pride in their Jewishness, despite the difficulties it created for them. If he were to go into politics, Disraeli had no choice other than to officially become a Christian: When he was young, Jews couldn't sit in Parliament. He would always carefully observe the rituals of his new religion, but of course all of England thought of him as a Jew (and therefore an outsider) anyway. Eventually, though, as Adam Kirsch points out in his recent biography of Disraeli, "He had been in politics for so long that he was now accepted as part of the establishment."

Like Disraeli, Sarah—publicly identified, and maligned, as a Jew through the first decades of her career—eventually escaped the specifics of her personal history to become a national icon, so that by the 1890s, the public apparently didn't find it anomalous or blasphemous that this scandalous "Jewess" was impersonating Joan of Arc. She called herself a Roman Catholic, but again as with Disraeli, formal religion was clearly more an afterthought in her life than a central concern. To both of them, Jewishness was a matter of race, not belief.

Émile Zola   Captain Alfred Dreyfus

1905—a year before the ultimate exoneration of Captain Dreyfus—the subject remained incendiary. Lysiane Bernhardt, in
her biography of her grandmother, recounts a bizarre scene
that took place in that year at another of the obligatory Sunday
lunches. Among the cast of characters: Clairin and Abbéma,
Meyer, the Charpentiers (publishers), and Édouard Geoffroy,
Simone's godfather, who had been a dedicated anti-Dreyfusard:

> The luncheon was proceeding gaily when suddenly the
> name Dreyfus was mentioned, referring to the manager
> of one of the big Paris shops. There was a moment of
> tension. Remember that there was no question of the
> Dreyfus of the "affair," but merely of a Dreyfus who had
> just died in an accident. Then Geoffroy muttered: "It's
> a pity it wasn't the traitor." Georges Clairin told him

to hold his tongue, and my grandmother exclaimed:
"We're not going to start that again!" My father
told Clairin not to be rude to Geoffroy; my mother
implored my father to be quiet. The Charpentiers began
to gesticulate . . . in short, it started all over again!
The butler no longer dared pass the dishes. Geoffroy
accidentally knocked the salad all over Abbéma with his
elbow. My sister began to giggle nervously. My grandmother poured me out another bumper of white wine,
then, at a remark by my father (her son), she broke
her plate in two. Her son (my father) took offense at this
and got up and began to pull my mother away from
the table by the hand. Then my grandmother broke my
plate on Geoffroy's arm and Geoffroy became purple
with fury. The Charpentiers got up and the whole party
scattered with screams of rage . . .

And so tragedy dissolved into farce.

XVIII

FROM THE TIME Sarah was established, she lived in a succession of splendidly decorated houses, surrounded by all the orna-mentalia and exotica of the high Victorian period. Her rooms were stuffed with furniture, rugs, draperies, mirrors, paint-ings (many of herself), busts (many *by* herself), velvet tapestries, immense vases, curiosities picked up on her travels. She never stopped acquiring them, but then when she'd run out of mon-ey—extravagant failed productions, lavish generosity (Maurice, as always), elegant houses built to her own designs—she'd once again cheerfully sell everything, get back on her feet, and start acquiring all over again. She had an enormous staff—cooks, maids, butlers, secretaries, coachmen, gardeners—to whom she hated paying wages but loved making extravagant gifts. The famous menagerie remained in a constant state of flux. Her close friend the English artist W. Graham Robertson tells us, "The tiger cub I never found attractive, though lovely to look upon. 'Don't hold him near your face,' said Sarah as she handed the formidable baby to me to nurse. 'He has a way of dabbing at your eyes.'" On the other hand, "The most fascinating of the pets was the lynx, a really lovable beast who ranged about the house at his will and was gentle, affectionate as well as graceful: the mysterious white-robed figure of Sarah coming down the steps into her studio with the lynx gliding noiselessly beside her was so suggestive of Circe that one looked about for the pigs."

Early on, Sarah had a little place near Le Havre where she went to rest up. In August 1894 she came upon a *big* place that would change her life. During a holiday with some of the inner circle on the Atlantic coast of Brittany, she took a day trip to the rugged, dramatic island nearby known as Belle-Île. They saw some of the sights, they had a pleasant lunch at an inn, and they were driven to the Point des Poulains, the very northwest tip of the island, where they came upon an isolated lighthouse, a wild sea, immense rocks . . . and a little abandoned fort. Through the spray and mist Sarah saw a sign: "Fort for sale." It was a *coup de foudre*. "My friend," she shouted to Georges Clairin, "I've got something important to tell you! All this belongs to me! I'm the owner of a fort! What do you say to that?" Instructing their guide to help make the necessary arrangements, she triumphantly rejoined her friends with the happy news: "I've bought the fort! We'll spend all our summers here." With Sarah, between the desire and the act fell no shadow.

By November the papers were signed: For three thousand francs, the fort and a modest amount of land around it were hers. Considering that she had recently returned from an American tour with three *million* francs, this was hardly an extravagance. The extravagance was to come. Over the years, she increased her holdings: land here, land there, a manor house called Penhoët that was within view and had been turned into

Above: a pencil drawing by Sarah of the fort at Belle-Île; and below, the manor house called Penhoët

Top, Sarah being greeted at Penhoët by, left to right, Reynaldo Hahn, her long-suffering secretary Pitou, Clairin, and Abbéma; above left, rock climbing with Clairin; above right, on the tennis court

a hotel, a farm where she could raise chickens, cows, and sheep and grow produce—the Marie Antoinette touch. She built bungalows for her loved ones—for Clairin, for Abbéma, for Maurice and his family, then for each of the granddaughters when they grew up. The fort, of course, had to be made habitable—windows in place of slits in the walls, for instance. A studio. A tennis court. A donkey cart. Her dozen or so dogs, including the matched pair, Cassis and Vermouth. Her parrots. Her frightening bird of prey, known as Le Grand Duc. Comfortable quarters for the endless stream of guests. A white banner flying over the fort proclaiming her initials, *SB*, and the inevitable *Quand même*. All told, she spent four million francs on her three thousand–franc investment, and it proved to be one of the happiest investments of her life.

All the testimony reveals an idyllic fun-filled life at Belle-Île, with Sarah at her most relaxed, her gayest, her most joyous. In the dozen summers before the amputation she was out on the rocks at dawn, paddling in the Atlantic, shrimping with nets, shooting sea birds. Lunch, or an extravagant picnic, was the main event of the day. Then siesta, followed by vigorous afternoon activities.

Reynaldo Hahn, one of her favorites, left a convincing account of life at Belle-Île, where he was installed almost annually (years earlier he had visited the island with his then-lover, Marcel Proust):

> In the afternoon, Sarah, refreshed and full of energy,
> would go fishing or play tennis. The game was an
> ordeal for her opponents as it was their duty to place
> the ball where she could reach it easily, for although she
> had a good serve and a strong return, it did not amuse
> her to run about, as she had problems with her right
> knee. Maurice, who was a marvelous player, was a past
> master at this. Clairin and Sarah's old friend Geoffroy
> managed fairly well, but their frequent lapses elicited
> furious curses from Sarah. [Her young friend Suze Rueff

put it this way: "It has to be admitted that Sarah was
a bad loser. . . . To lose at tennis, at dominoes or cards,
infuriated her. She would cheat and resort to the most
childish tricks in her efforts to win; she knew it
was idiotic, but *c'est plus fort que moi;* she could not
help herself."]

    At dinner one night, passionate discussions
about nothing. Dominoes. Then I go to the piano
and play the gypsy song from *Carmen.* Maurice tries
a Spanish dance; his daughters imitate him. I speed
up the tempo. Suddenly, old Geoffroy, in knicker-
bockers and a Norfolk jacket, leaps up and improvises
a mad fandango. With unbelievable "go," he executes
dizzying twists and turns, backbends and cartwheels,
shaking with laughter. We all laugh till it hurts.
Sarah, her head in her hands, laughs till she weeps,
sobs, and hiccoughs. Gasping for air, she leans
back, her eyes closed. Then, just as she calms down,
she bursts out all over again.

Maurice Baring: "During the whole time I stayed there
[at Belle-Île], Sarah never mentioned the theatre, acting, or actors. . . . She was irresistibly comic at times, full of bubbling
gaiety and spirits, and an admirable mimic. . . . What struck me
most about her, when I saw her in private life, was her radiant
and ever-present common sense. There was no nonsense about
her, no pose, and no posturing. She was completely natural.
She took herself for granted as being the greatest actress in
the world, as Queen Victoria took it for granted that she was
Queen of England. She took it for granted and passed on."

    The idylls at Belle-Île lasted until 1922, a year before her
death, when Sarah suddenly decided it was all too much for her
and, without a moment's hesitation, sold it—as precipitously as
she had bought it.

    The first dozen or so Belle-Île years coincided with other
felicitous aspects of her life: the triumphs of *Hamlet, L'Aiglon,*

Lucien Guitry

and *La Sorcière*, and the publication of *Ma Double Vie*, which enjoyed a considerable popular and critical success. Max Beerbohm: "Hers is a volcanic nature, as we know, and hers has been a volcanic career; and nothing of this volcanicism [*sic*] is lost in her description of it"; he went on to celebrate the book's "peculiar fire and salt . . . the rushing spontaneity that stamps it, for every discriminating reader, as Sarah's own."

And then there were the gratifications of her collaboration with two of the finest actors of her time.

In Lucien Guitry she had at last a partner whom she both admired and trusted. He was big, masculine, a ladies' man, both subtle and commanding as an actor. After their brief pro forma fling, he went on to act with her over several decades— in *La Princesse lointaine* in 1895, as the original Flambeau in *L'Aiglon* in 1900, in *Phèdre, Gismonda, La Tosca*. She entrusted the management of her theater to him while she toured, and to the end of her life was close to him and his family, particularly his extraordinary son, the phenomenally successful actor-writer-director Sacha—more or less the French equivalent of

Noël Coward. In her perceptive book *Madame Sarah*, the actress Cornelia Otis Skinner described Lucien's manner of acting as "one of naturalness and a powerful simplicity that came as a startling innovation to a period of artificiality and superfluous gesture. His magnetism was phenomenal and when he walked onto a stage one was struck by a Presence as when Chaliapin made one of his astonishing entrances." And she quotes the popular playwright Henri Bataille, who said of him, "Guitry is the first real man who has trodden the stage."

No one ever called Sarah's other important colleague of this period "a real man." The brilliant onstage persona of the exotic Édouard de Max—born in Romania to a Jewish doctor and a fake Eastern princess—was almost as exaggerated as the figure he cut in private life. (He was Nero in *Britannicus*, the wicked priest in *Gismonda*, the Grand Inquisitor in *La Samaritaine*.) Max was utterly louche, but also loyal, funny, and good-natured. At the center of a coterie of exquisite homosexuals, master of ceremonies at various kinds of bacchanalias (he liked to shower his naked young male guests with gold coins), he adored Sarah, and she him. Among his acolytes were André Gide and the sixteen-year-old Jean Cocteau, who later would describe him as "a prince of *comme-il-ne-faut-pas*." (He was also known as *Le Monsieur aux camélias*.) The important thing is that, unlike so many of her earlier leading men, he was a true artist.

"De Max was a brilliant tragedian," wrote Cocteau. "Like Madame [Isadora] Duncan and Bernhardt, he knew nothing of codes and formulas. He sought, he invented. He embarrassed. He raved. You felt somehow responsible for his mistakes. You didn't dare look at your neighbors; you were sweating buckets. Suddenly you were ashamed of your embarrassment. Cries of 'ssh!' stifled the last laugh. De Max, a fist clenched in rage, overcame the ridicule and trampled it down. His haughtiness bore it away and bore you with it, at full speed.

"Can I ever forget his Nero in *Britannicus*?—an operetta

Édouard de Max

Nero in emerald monocle and train, who keeps you from picturing Nero in any other way."

Max's most dubious contribution to Sarah's life was a young actor named Lou Tellegen (born Isidore Van Dammelen to a Dutch general and a Greek dancer), whom he proposed to her as a substitute for himself when he chose not to be bored on yet another American tour. The year was 1910. Tellegen had a notorious history which, later, he would elaborate on and embellish in his memoir *Women Have Been Kind*. (Dorothy Parker, reviewing it in *Vanity Fair*, said that they should have added the words *"of Dumb"* to the title.) Actually, men had been kind, too—Max, for one. Tellegen was twenty-nine at the time—a

mere thirty-seven years younger than Sarah—and exception-
ally handsome, though not much of an actor. (Well, that never
worried her—remember Angelo and Damala.) She met him and
hired him on the spot at an exorbitant salary, securing his services for a four-year period, and carrying him off to New York
for her upcoming American tour—all this without ever having
seen him act. In America he was given the major young-male
leads, was (needless to say) installed in her private railroad carriage, and was seen with her everywhere, with the result that he
became an object of derision to the Parisian public and of loath-
ing to her family. She even considered marrying him. From the
Los Angeles Examiner, November 23, 1911: "The secret is out in
Paris that Madame Sarah Bernhardt is going to marry M. Tellegen, her young leading man." This "diable de Tellegen," the
story goes on, is a real "*bel animal*, a big fellow with the jaws of
a bulldog and the teeth of a young wolf: what a splendid mate
he might have been, half a century ago, to Sarah, the 'panther
of love,' as they used to call her in the Latin Quarter." She may
have been a panther, but "He is a lion," she's quoted as saying,
"eyeing him between half-closed lids and with a slight quiver
of her delicate nostrils; 'Ah, it is wonderful to be so strong;
women love strong men.'" The next day, in the *Chicago Examiner:* "Mme. Sarah Bernhardt says that she is not going to marry again." Not long before she encountered Tellegen, she was
asked by an outspoken friend when she planned to give up love.
"With my dying breath!" she answered. "I intend to live as I
have always lived." (She had proudly told Suze Rueff, "I have
been one of the greatest *amoureuses* of my time.")

Tellegen seems from this distance to have been an easygoing, relatively decent fellow (unlike Damala); certainly he was
unreservedly adulatory about Sarah in his book, and grateful.
"Every moment I worked with her I knew the best that the theatre can give, and, remembering the most glorious four years of
my life, my eyes filled with tears and my heart again cried out
'Madame! Grande Madame! I am so alone without you!'"

Lou Tellegen

She put him into her movies—as Essex in her *Queen
Elizabeth*, as Armand in her *La Dame aux camélias*—and then
advised him to go back to America, where he was well liked.
Tellegen's Essex looks ludicrous today, but the prestige of having co-starred with Bernhardt plus his looks paved the way
for him. He went to Hollywood, had a successful career there
in silent films, married the great opera diva Geraldine Farrar, married three other kind women, and ended up—his looks
gone, and with a bad drug habit—committing suicide by stabbing himself seven times with a pair of sewing scissors. Sardou
could have written it—and Sarah would have played him.

XIX

IN STARK contrast to the felicities of Belle-Île and Tellegen were Sarah's declining health and increasingly reduced mobility. She had suffered a knee injury decades before, falling on the deck of a ship that was taking her back to Europe from one of her early American tours and making things worse by refusing to let the ship's doctor attend to her. (It's also possible that the original cause of the problem went back to the damage she did to herself in her early childhood when she flung herself—if, indeed, she did—in front of her Aunt Rosine's carriage.) The damage was exacerbated when at the climax of a performance of *La Tosca*, she threw herself from the parapet of the Sant'Angelo prison and there was no mattress in place to break her fall. From that time on she lived in pain, which eventually grew so agonizing that in 1915 she determined that she could no longer live with it: She would have her leg amputated. Those closest to her were horrified, but as always she faced reality coolly and decisively, telling the weeping Maurice that if he couldn't bear the idea of amputation, she would commit suicide: It was up to him to decide. He capitulated. Reassuring her beloved Dr. Pozzi that she would be fine after the deed was done—"I'll give lecture tours, I'll give lessons, and be gay. I don't want to lose my gaiety"—she insisted that the operation take place immediately. Pozzi, who couldn't bear the idea of her possibly dying under his hand, appointed a young surgeon, a Dr. Denucé, to take over.

Her bravery never faltered. After firing off telegrams to her friends—"So happy—my leg is cut off tomorrow"; "Tomorrow they're taking my leg off. Think of me and book me some lectures for April"—she went under the knife. The young woman who was her anesthetist was a perceptive if highly indiscreet observer:

> At 10 A.M. the great artist was wheeled into the operating room. She was dressed in a white satin peignoir and

Sarah at the front, in the litter chair she devised after her amputation

swathed in pink crêpe-de-chine veils. She seemed very calm. She sent for her son, Maurice, who came in to embrace her. During this tender scene she was heard to say "Au revoir, my beloved, my Maurice, au revoir. There, there, I'll be back soon." It was the same voice I had heard in *La Tosca, La Dame aux camélias, L'Aiglon*. Turning to Denucé she said: "My darling, give me a kiss." Then to me, "Mademoiselle, I am in your hands. Promise you'll really put me to sleep. Let's go, quickly, quickly." In all this one couldn't help seeing the tragedienne putting on an act. I felt I was at the theater, except that I myself had a role in the painful drama.

The operation succeeded and her recovery was long and painful but complete—except that her right leg was gone from above the knee. She tried a wooden leg, but found it unacceptable. Crutches were not an option. Eventually, she devised a white sedan chair—a kind of litter—in which she was carried around for the rest of her life. A young American friend visited her bedside soon after the amputation, and Sarah spoke casually of the physical difficulties she would have to overcome in order

Sarah in her antiwar film *Les Mères Françaises*

to act again. "Her tone was matter-of-fact, without a touch of plaintiveness. . . . 'There is always a way. You remember my motto "Quand même"? In case of necessity I shall have myself strapped to the scenery.'" And Sarah repeats the famous last words of a man who was dying at the height of her notoriety: "At least I won't have to hear about Sarah Bernhardt any longer."

(A comic-macabre touch: After the operation, P. T. Barnum apparently cabled her, offering ten thousand dollars for her amputated leg, to which she is said to have replied, "If it's my right leg you want, see the doctors; if it's the left leg, see my manager in New York." From the famous American producer Daniel Frohman comes another version of this story—take your pick: "Shortly after she had recovered from the amputation of her leg, she received a cable from a man I knew—the manager of a department of the Pan-American Exposition in San Francisco. He had the temerity to ask for her permission to exhibit her leg at the Exposition, offering her $100,000 which she could present to any charity she chose. She cabled back two words: 'Which leg?'")

The operation, its costs partly covered by the Rothschilds, had taken place in Bordeaux. Late in the previous year, some months after World War I had broken out, she had been convinced by the government to leave Paris—her friend Georges Clemenceau, not yet premier, had learned that she was on a list of potential hostages which the Germans had drawn up in anticipation of capturing the city. Returning now to the capital, which appeared to be out of danger, she threw herself into war work. Since she could no longer run a hospital as she had forty-odd years earlier during the previous German war, she determined to perform for the men at the front. Again the government intervened, but this time to no avail: In the autumn of 1915, in her seventies, she set out to entertain the troops.

One of the most distinguished of France's young actresses at the time, Béatrix Dussane (later to be an important historian of twentieth-century French theater), was chosen to accompany her, and has left a moving account of their adventures, and of Sarah herself at this time.

Dussane is ushered into Sarah's white boudoir, "where I see in the depths of a huge armchair an extraordinary creature: a thousand rumples of satin and lace topped with a tousled red coiffeur, ageless features whose wrinkles are caked over with makeup. It was upsetting, and a bit sad; she seems so small, so damaged, the great, the radiant Sarah! A little heap of cinders."

Then the miracle occurs. "For two hours she rehearsed, went back over her lines, made cuts, ordered tea, cross-examined me about our trip, was in turn enthusiastic, moved, and amused. She saw everything, understood everything, anticipated everything. All this time the little heap of cinders never stopped emitting sparks! I feel this has occurred ever since she came into the world, and will continue forever. Beneath the painted and tinseled decrepitude of the old actress there burns an inextinguishable sun."

They perform in an open marketplace to three thousand soldiers, many of them wounded (and most of them hoping for a movie). At the end of her recitation she cries *Aux armes*, the Marseillaise is sung, and the men all stand and cheer. The two actresses perform on the terrace of a deserted château, in hospital wards, in mess tents, in a ruined barn packed to the rafters. Dussane:

> I witness the genius of Sarah and I witness her bravery. . . .
> Once I had to help her dress. She went from chair
> to table leaning on my arm or hopping on her poor,
> seventy-two-year-old leg, saying with that infectious
> laugh of hers, "Look, I'm just like a guinea hen!" The
> way she ignored her handicap was beautiful—a victory of
> the spirit over the failing flesh. One didn't pity her, one
> admired her. I shall always remember her, that old
> woman of genius, clopping along in her sedan chair or
> on her one leg, ready to give her flaming heart to those
> brave men who were fighting and dying for us.

(Later, in the *Ladies' Home Journal*, Sarah would refer to this episode as "the supreme adventure of my life.")

Several weeks later she was back, this time with Lysiane, playing in towns along the Marne and at Reims, against the backdrop of the damaged cathedral. She went to a small town that was bombed regularly—but not the day she was there. She begged to be allowed to go into the trenches, and was only with difficulty persuaded not to. She was once again doing her best for her country. Surely if she hadn't (finally) been granted the Légion d'Honneur in 1914, she would have been awarded it now.

It was presumably during these trips to the war zone that some of the scenes from her film *Les Mères françaises* were filmed—certainly the moment in which she stands outside the Reims cathedral at midnight (the sandbags protecting the exterior of the cathedral were removed for fifteen minutes—Reims was under bombardment—so that the scene could be shot), and possibly also the scenes in which she's half-carried through the trenches, under fire, as she desperately searches for her wounded son. The film was distributed in 1917 to great success both in France and abroad—an antiwar statement and at the same time an effective piece of propaganda intended to rally French morale. For once Sarah isn't doing a star turn but is partaking in a realistic drama about the people of a single village whose lives are crushed by the war. Indeed, the heroine of *Les Mères françaises* is not so much Sarah as "La France." Always, Sarah was three things above all others: an actress, a mother, and a patriot. No wonder, then, that she chose to participate in *Les Mères françaises*. Besides, it was written by her old colleague and flame Jean Richepin.

In the fall of 1916, as usual needing money but also determined to help persuade America to join the war, Sarah set out on her ninth and last American tour. Given the loss of her leg, she could no longer cope with full-length plays but made a selection of short scenes or acts—an act from *La Dame*, for instance—that she could perform in vaudeville halls as well as legitimate theaters. She would go to ninety-nine cities in fourteen months including, on one stretch of the itinerary, Salem, Portland, Bridgeport, New Haven, Worcester, Springfield, Pittsfield, Albany, Port Huron, Saginaw, Flint, Lansing, Battle Creek, and Grand Rapids. A review in the *Poughkeepsie Eagle-News* gives us the flavor of these performances:

> The program consisted of two scenes: "La Morte de Cleopatre" and the trial scene from the "Merchant of Venice" with three other numbers to fill out the evening's entertainment. All the lines were spoken in French but this did not seem to dampen anyone's ardor or enthusiasm and at the close of the performance this enthusiasm was almost overwhelming. Madame Bernhardt had to respond again and again to curtain calls while the entire audience stood up to applaud.
>
> Both the scenes were so arranged that it was not necessary for Madame Bernhardt to move about at all. In "Cleopatre" she reclined on a couch surrounded by several Egyptian maidens and it was only necessary for her to stand two or three times during the action of the piece. In the trial scene from the "Merchant of Venice" which opens sometime before the appearance of Portia, the curtain dropped for an instant while the entrance was effected.
>
> The scenic effects were very good indeed and while in "Cleopatre" the lighting was dim and it was hard to see Madame Bernhardt distinctly, she stood the glare of the brightest of lights in the "Merchant of Venice" and did not appear any older than Portia should.

On this same tour she also appeared in the trial scene as Shylock. The *Brooklyn Eagle:* "It is a fiendishly cruel and vengeful Jew. . . . It glares with diabolic hatred at the Christian merchant, his eyes glistening like those of Cleopatra's asp in anticipating his gory vengeance." "The lines of this Shylock's face are all hard, rectangular," said the *Christian Science Monitor.* "On the head is a mop of stringy gray hair and on the chin a short thin pointed gray beard." Surely alternating the roles of Portia and Shylock was the first, and last, such parlay in the history of the theater.

The tour was interrupted by a recurrence of the serious uremic malady that had plagued her on and off for years. Now, in New York, an ocean away from her family, she was close to death. A remarkable series of headlines in the *New York Times* tells the story.

April 17, 1917:
SARAH BERNHARDT MAY GO UNDER KNIFE

April 18:
STAGE STARS JOIN IN ALLIED BENEFIT
Bernhardt Sends a Kiss from Her Bed in
Mt. Sinai Hospital to Great Audience

Also April 18:
SARAH BERNHARDT IS OPERATED UPON —
SURGEONS RESORT TO ONLY HOPE OF SAVING LIFE OF
ACTRESS SUFFERING FROM INFECTED KIDNEY —
RESTS EASILY AFTERWARD
Dr. Leo Buerger Wields the Knife in Mt. Sinai Hospital
with Five Physicians in Attendance

April 20:
MME. BERNHARDT BETTER
Actress's Marvelous Vitality Gives Hope of Her Recovery

April 21:
MME. BERNHARDT GAINS
Hope Now for Her Recovery—Queen Alexandra
Sends Message

April 22:
Bernhardt's Condition Unchanged

April 25:
Mme. Bernhardt Steadily Improves

April 28:
Mme. Bernhardt Gaining Daily

It was coverage that would normally be accorded a president, a king . . . or a queen.

In Paris, Maurice and the rest of the family were tortured with anxiety, and he at once set out for New York with Lysiane and his second wife, Marcelle, to be with Sarah while she recovered. Soon she was back on the road, with Lysiane staying on to look after her. Accompanying them in Sarah's private railroad carriage was a new menagerie—a Pekingese, an Airedale, and a lion cub named Hernani II, which, Lysiane tells us, "drank milk soup and gazed at me with sad, gold-flecked eyes. It grew larger week by week, clawed me to the bone, and climbed up hotel curtains. . . . Soon Hernani was eating raw meat and loudly crunching bones." It also "made large messes, always at luncheon time and always on the carpet." After six months, Hernani II was reluctantly returned to the circus.

Apart from her stage appearances, Sarah was exerting all her energies to rouse the American public to the Allied cause. Interviews, impassioned pleas from the stage ("I would rather be a private soldier fighting for France than to be Bernhardt— that's how I feel about it!") followed by recitations of "La Marseillaise," speeches at Red Cross rallies and other public events. She was living up to her reputation in America as "the greatest missionary whom France or any other country has sent abroad."

She was also speaking out on other issues, among them women ("For a woman there are three subjects and three alone, no matter how many varieties one may mention. They are love, maternity, and sorrow") and racism, praising a suffragette convention for standing by a black woman who was being kept from joining them in the hotel where the conference was being held: "I think that the ostracism in which blacks are held by the whites is odious."

Her opinions were solicited on everything, and she never hesitated to give them. Only on the delicate subject of religion was she untypically silent, but in 1917 a journalist friend wrote in *Munsey's* magazine, "Though by race a Jewess, like

Rachel her great forerunner, she is a professing Catholic. How orthodox she is, I dare not say; but from what she has at various times confessed to me in informal talks, I should judge that her religious views may best be described as 'broad.' That she has genuine faith in the existence of God I feel certain. But I should regard her less as a Catholic than as a spiritualist and a romantic idealist."

At last, in the fall of 1918—solvent again and desperate to be back home with Maurice—she boarded a ship for France. The German U-boats were still prowling, but when the ship's captain offered to assign two sailors to stand by her in case of torpedoes, she replied indignantly, "They'll be needed elsewhere. Young lives are more important than my old one." The ship docked at Bordeaux on November 11, 1918, and Maurice rushed through the welcoming crowds to reach her. "*Maman*," he cried. "They've signed the armistice! The war is over!"

XX

THE YEARS before and after the war were filled not only with a constant supply of new plays, revivals, touring, managing her theater, and enjoying Belle-Île but with various occupations that she took up, usually successfully. She was, for instance, always writing, not only the several silly novels like *Petite Idole* that she turned out almost overnight for some ready (and, as always, needed) cash, but the torrent of letters (almost illegible) that issued from her daily and which have the energy, the fluency, the dash of her memoirs, plus the immediacy that daily correspondence confers. Alas, her letters haven't been collected, and the job would be a forbidding one—just tracking them down around the world would be a formidable task. (For instance, in a family archive in northern Italy there's a stash of correspondence with Puccini's librettists involving their work

on *Tosca*, and undoubtedly there are dozens of other uninves-
tigated archives.) Her letters to Maurice alone would probably
fill a book—if you could decipher them.

In her final three years she dictated a series of reflections
on acting that were then edited, arranged, and, a year after her
death, published in a book called *The Art of the Theatre*. Several
extended passages contain highly specific instructions—for instance, on makeup: "A dark woman should always expose a part
of her forehead, in order to lighten her face. She should not put
black around the eyes, but only lengthen the eye with a chestnut-
colored pencil, never a black pencil." But her advice is mostly
general—the actor must live his role, etc. She still, however, fifty
years after leaving the Conservatoire, is railing against its for-
mulaic approach and counterproductive rules, and demanding
that someone—the government?—step forward and modernize
the curriculum. Nor had her disdain for the Comédie-Française
abated. Verneuil tells us that the two of them were driving past
the theater on a Sunday and observed about a hundred people
standing outside the entrance. Sarah: "Who are all those people?" Verneuil: "They're waiting for the actors to come out."
Sarah (with a silvery little laugh): "In order to kill them?"

As it happened, back in 1906 she had been asked to teach
at the Conservatoire—a relationship that lasted exactly one
term. She was an actress, not a pedagogue, and she was so much
a lesson unto herself that it wasn't possible to learn from her example; Sarah Bernhardt was the last, as well as the first, of her
kind. "Her position at the Conservatoire was never supported,"
one commentator writes, "her judgments were overruled, her
original methods unappreciated." She did, however, give some
private classes for a while, and among her students was a young
half-French, half-English girl named May Agate, whose French
was perfect and who did indeed become a successful actress in
England later on. (Her mother was an old friend of Sarah's, and
her brother James Agate became one of England's most influential theater critics.) How did Sarah teach? May tells us:

We did no exercises, read no tomes, absorbed no conventions. In fact, "la Tradition" (words spoken by her with an infinity of scorn) was her *bête noire*. She admitted nothing which did not spring from truth and sincerity.

She never moved from her chair to demonstrate. She would explain, lecture to us, illustrate by anecdote—in short, make the characters into living people for us, giving us the thought behind the words ("The author has forgotten to write that in," she would often say)—indeed, everything except show us how. I am sure this was deliberate and not attributable to infirmity, for I often saw her show an actor at rehearsal how to time a move. But with students never. It all had to be done through heart, mind, and understanding—not just the quickest way, which is by imitation. That has no lasting results. . . . What appealed to me in her teaching was the extraordinary application of common sense to the interpretation of every line, so that it never ceased to be a human being speaking, however flowery the language might be. It was a simply devastating method for those who would have got away with a conventional rendering if they could. You had to think, and think hard, all the time.

She was also, one has to remember, running a major theater, which in her case meant paying attention to every possible detail. Anecdotes abound that demonstrate how she took upon herself any task that needed doing, however minor. May Agate provides one example: "So insistent was she upon correctness of detail that she was not above 'breaking down' a pair of new boots worn by a child super at a dress rehearsal. She immediately sent for the boots and got busy with wet Fuller's earth and greasepaint to represent mud, which she herself worked into the offending leather until it offended her no longer! This is no hearsay—I saw her do it."

In 1899, her beloved Edmond Rostand conveyed what her average workday was like:

A brougham stops at a door; a woman, enveloped in furs, jumps out, threads her way with a smile through the crowd attracted by the jingling of the bell on the harness, and mounts a winding stair; plunges into a room crowded with flowers and heated like a hothouse; throws her little beribboned handbag with its apparently inexhaustible contents into one corner, and her bewinged hat into another; takes off her furs and instantaneously dwindles to a mere scabbard of white silk; rushes on to a dimly lighted stage and immediately puts life into a whole crowd of listless, yawning, loitering folk; dashes backward and forward, inspiring every one with her own feverish energy; goes into the prompter's box, arranges her scenes, points out the proper gesture and intonation, rises up in wrath and insists on everything being done over again; shouts with fury; sits down, smiles, drinks tea, and begins to rehearse her own part; draws tears from case-hardened actors who thrust their enraptured heads out of the wings to watch her; returns to her room, where the decorators are waiting, demolishes their plans and reconstructs them; collapses, wipes her brow with a lace handkerchief and thinks of fainting; suddenly rushes up to the fifth floor, invades the premises of the astonished costumier, rummages in the wardrobes, makes up a costume, pleats it and adjusts it; returns to her room and teaches the *figurantes* how to dress their hair; has a play read to her while she makes bouquets; listens to hundreds of letters, weeps over some tale of misfortune, and opens the inexhaustible little chinking handbag; confers with an English *perruquier*; returns to the stage to superintend the lighting of a scene, violently criticizes the lamps and reduces the electrician to a state of temporary insanity; sees a super who had blundered the day before, remembers it, and overwhelms him with her indignation; returns to her room for dinner; sits down to table, splendidly pale with fatigue; ruminates over her plans; eats with peals of Bohemian laughter; has no time to finish; dresses for

the evening performance while the manager reports from
the other side of the curtain; acts with all her heart
and soul; discusses business between the acts; remains at
the theater after the performance, and makes arrangements until three o'clock in the morning; does not make
up her mind to go until she sees her staff respectfully
endeavoring to keep awake; gets into her carriage;
huddles herself into her furs and anticipates the delights
of lying down and resting at last; bursts out laughing
on remembering that someone is waiting to read her a
five-act play; returns home, listens to the piece, becomes
excited, weeps, accepts it, finds she cannot sleep and
takes advantage of the opportunity to study a part! . . .
This is the Sarah I have always known. I never made the
acquaintance of the Sarah with the coffin and the
alligators. The only Sarah I know is the one who works.

There were those, however, for whom she was a figure of
fun. In 1890 the up-and-coming cabaret star Yvette Guilbert,
in the wake of the Sardou-Bernhardt *Cléopâtre*, unleashed a satirical song called "Le Petit Serpent de Sarah" about the poor
little asp who couldn't find anything to sink its teeth into when
clasped to Sarah's un-bosom. Everyone but Sarah was amused.
Perhaps she recognized in Guilbert a nature as avid and determined as her own. (By 1893 it was reported that Yvette's "success in Parisian concert halls has been so great that Russia is
longing for her at Sarah Bernhardt prices.")

Through the years their paths crossed several times,
with varying degrees of warmth and bitchiness, until in 1917
Yvette visited Sarah in New York's Mount Sinai Hospital. In
her memoirs, she writes,

I found her outrageously made up and powdered, her
eyes thick with black, her lips scarlet, her red hair
crimped and fluffed up—a lion in bed! She terrified me.
My God, my God! Not to be able to be oneself while in
fever and agony; always to be wearing a mask and

deploying stage effects, and to deceive whom? She talked about her son. "If only he'd come," she said, "they could operate . . . if only he'd come," and a great tenderness shone in her eyes. At one moment she held my hand on her eiderdown, and said: "You are really kind, Yvette. . . . I thank you for coming . . . " I had to leave because I could feel the emotion rising in my throat and was afraid I was going to weep. It wrung my heart to see her. I wanted to scrub off her greasepaint and restore the beauty to her sad face. I kissed her and fled.

A touching scene, if somewhat patronizing, but Guilbert's notion of Sarah letting herself go even in the face of possible death reveals the utter failure on her part to understand whom she was dealing with.

A more serious incompatibility of temperaments was that between Sarah and Eleonora Duse, the one formidable rival of the latter part of Sarah's career. Their encounters constitute the typical comedy of dueling divas, but there were also basic differ-

Caricature by Léandre of Sarah sparring with Yvette Guilbert

ences both in the way they acted and the way they lived. Duse's reputation as a profound natural artist, spurning makeup and affectation, plumbing the depths of human sorrow, drew Sarah's scorn, while Duse, who had been inspired in her youth by seeing Sarah act in Turin ("No one spoke of anyone but her. . . . One woman had accomplished that! My reaction was to feel liberated, to feel I had the right to do whatever I wanted to . . . "), cautiously avoided Paris long after she was adulated everywhere else that counted. Apart from her natural trepidation about challenging the most famous actress in the world on her own turf, there was a problem of repertory. Duse, of course, was famous as the apostle of the new—Ibsen, in particular, but also Sudermann and her lover D'Annunzio—but she also shared many of Sarah's roles: *La Dame aux camélias, Fédora, La Femme de Claude, Adrienne Lecouvreur.* In 1897, when Duse finally decided the time was right to brave Paris, Sarah offered her the Renaissance theater (according to Sarah, free of charge; according to Duse, at exorbitant expense—and, to add insult to injury, without access to Sarah's superb dressing room, which was officially "closed for repairs").

Before Duse opened, Sarah invited her to a performance of *La Samaritaine*, and Duse jumped up in her box and stood every time Sarah entered, distracting the audience. One up to Duse. But on *her* opening night, in *La Dame*, Sarah watched from her own box magnificently gowned and bejeweled, in sharp contrast to Duse's very un-courtesan-like and nervous Marguerite. "What do you think?" a reporter asked Sarah. "One of the best," she smiled.

Eventually, they both performed at a benefit to raise money toward a statue of Dumas *fils*, to whom each of them owed so much. But relations went on deteriorating, as Duse's success grew. Sarah, however, got in the last shot. She not only scooped up D'Annunzio's new play, *La città morta*, which Duse had planned to premiere in Italy, but she scooped up D'Annunzio himself—to her, a tiny fling meant to humiliate her rival; to Duse, an emotional disaster. (By then Duse should have been used to her lover's sadistic behavior.) When the poet first came to call on Sarah, he tactlessly cried, "You are sublime, madame! Positively D'Annunzian!" As Gold and Fizdale remark, "What was meant to flatter her did not go down well, for Sarah, with a rather healthy ego of her own, preferred to think of herself as Bernhardtian."

There were accusations and counteraccusations over Duse's Paris season: Who took advantage of whom? Who slighted whom? Who came out on top? But how could it have been otherwise? Except in her memoirs, where she carefully explained that Duse was a great actress but not a great artist, Sarah was publicly polite. In private, she was less careful. To Reynaldo Hahn: "What a lovely head! That disdainful mouth, those white teeth, those eyes, smiling yet sad. And what charm! A great actress!" Then as an afterthought: "What a pity she's so pretentious!" In later years, at a moment when Duse was at low ebb, Sarah heard her name mentioned and asked disingenuously, "What ever became of that old lady?" "That old lady" was the younger of the two by fifteen years.

XXI

THE CONTRAST in acting styles between Sarah and Duse fascinated critics and audiences for decades, just as at the beginning of Sarah's career she was constantly held up in comparison to the glorious memory and reputation of Rachel. But Rachel had died young, in 1858, and Sarah never saw her act. They had had much in common—their Jewishness (openly mocked), their reckless and highly public amours, and of course their genius. But they were unalike in their acting. Rachel had such tragic power, so much command of the stage, that almost from the first moment she appeared at the Français she was its greatest star—a far cry from Sarah's early stumbling years. Her voice

Sarah's great predecessor Rachel, as Phèdre

Sarah's great rival Eleonora Duse, as La Dame aux camélias

was neither golden nor silver—it was bronze, and her presence was imposing, like that of a marble statue. Her preferred playwright was Corneille, with his stern call to duty rather than to love. Rachel was considered sublime as Phèdre, her crime the tragic flaw of a goddess, whereas Sarah's Phèdre was human, the victim of a woman's irresistible passion. You were in awe of Rachel, you suffered with Sarah.

The differences between them were not only the reflection of different temperaments; they also reflected a radical cultural change. Rachel was a classicist; Sarah was a child of the Romantic movement, and her theater was the theater of feelings, of rebellion, of the Self. Rachel dominated; Sarah, in her early years, appealed. But if she lacked command, she had several important advantages—the loveliness of her rather weak voice and her perfect articulation of verse. She may have resisted certain of the strictures of her professors at the Conservatoire, but she internalized the rules—how to speak, how to move. She could not be Rachel, but she didn't want to be: Everything must be *her* way. We have to remember that she began her training not as a girl desperate to act, for whom the stage was an irresistible attraction, but as a girl looking for a way out of a difficult domestic situation; there was no burning talent demanding to be expressed. Before she could become a successful actress, she had to *decide* to be an actress, and direct her will toward that goal. And, of course, once Sarah willed something, she had to achieve it, the greater the challenges, the better.

She also had, despite (because of?) her highly unconventional looks, a special allure. Her exaggerated thinness, her pale coloring, her exotic face, and her poetic charm set her off from every other actress once she had earned the right to assume roles appropriate to her. There was a touch of hysteria, perhaps even of danger, in her willingness to expose her emotions, to impose them on her audience. Yet her elegance of carriage, the charm of her voice, and her consummate taste in the delivery of her lines protected her from appearing uncomfortably aggressive.

Sarah's playwrights: clockwise from top left, Alexandre Dumas *fils*, Victorien Sardou, and Edmond Rostand

There is endless testimony about Sarah's acting—literally thousands of reviews by theater critics in Paris and around the world, hundreds of references by friends and colleagues to this or that performance, attempts by biographers and historians to suggest the qualities and effects of her work. But even apart from the fundamental difficulty of grasping the qualities of unrecorded performances of an earlier era, a particular problem stands in the way of our understanding what she was like on stage. Unlike so many actors who find a single path and continue along it, Sarah's tremendous work span—sixty years—taken together with her shifting approaches to her art, make it clear that she was a different actress at different times in her career, rather than one who simply improved or deteriorated. One of the ironies of her life is that at the start she is seen as the exemplar of a new realism in acting in contrast to the stylizations of Rachel, while thirty-five years later, *she* is disparaged as representing the stylized acting of the past, and Duse is the exemplar of a new realism.

Her early career at the Odéon, after she had passed beyond the status of beginner, depended on her genius for speaking verse combined with her fresh appeal: *Le Passant* revealed her androgynous charm, *Ruy Blas* her feminine elegance and distinction. At the Français, she began to assert her powers, triumphing in *Phèdre* and matching Mounet-Sully in strength and authority. Yet she was determined to cast off the requirements of the Français approach and forge a style that would proclaim her individuality.

Her range at that time may have extended from Chérubin in *Le Mariage de Figaro* to the old blind woman in *Rome Vaincue*, but one senses that these were amusing challenges for her rather than an expression of who she was as a woman and an actress. She was still proving something—to her mother, to Perrin, to Sarcey, to herself. Her confidence seems somehow tentative, partly, no doubt, because she understood the limitations of her voice. Again and again through the years critics pointed out the strain Sarah placed on it when she shouted or screamed. In the 1870s, while still at the Français, she developed her own tactic for dealing with this problem, speaking her lines so swiftly that frequently all meaning was lost, occasionally punctuating a passage delivered in a near-monotone with an explosive word or phrase. Audiences were excited by this practice, but Sarcey engaged in a twenty-year war with her over it, in 1879 writing:

> Mlle Sarah Bernhardt persists in a fault which we have already pointed out to her several times with no apparent effect. There are passages that she delivers . . . so rapidly that no one, not even those in the first rows of the orchestra, can understand a word she is saying. In the language of the theater, this is called *déblyage*. There is actually nothing wrong with *déblyage* if it serves to throw a particular passage into relief . . . *Déblyage*, however, must never reach the point where it is mere jabbering.

Four years later, he remarks that this device, which Sarah still clung to, "eventually savors of histrionic chicanery." By the mid-nineties, however, she had eradicated this blemish and began to be congratulated by the press for having abandoned *déblyage*.

There was also tension at the Français between its idea of an ensemble company of highly polished actors performing important plays and Sarah's natural inclination—her determination—to stand out. What she wanted, even if she didn't articulate it, was a series of vehicles for her unique personality. Yes, given her command of poetry and the radiance of her silvery voice, she could prevail as a Racinian princess, just as, with her exotic looks and enigmatic nature, she could hold her own against Sophie Croizette in inferior dramas like *Le Sphinx* and *L'Étrangère*, but these were not Bernhardt plays. Her dominance was even kept in check in *Hernani* and *Ruy Blas*—by the demands of Hugo's situations and the impact of Mounet-Sully playing opposite her. And so the ultimate Bernhardt style could not yet flower. When it did emerge, the contrast was soon apparent. You could say that the trajectory of Sarah Bernhardt's acting recapitulates the comparable (and contemporaneous) transformation in grand opera from bel canto to verismo. The decisive moment of change was 1880, when she left the Français and struck out on her own. The choices were now all hers, and at once she launched a new repertory in which the attraction was not the writer or the company but herself. (It was almost exactly the trajectory that Anna Pavlova would pursue thirty years later when she left first Russia, then Diaghilev's Ballets Russes, to circle the globe with her own company, in her own highly specialized repertory.) The three plays Sarah performed most frequently on her first American tour—*La Dame aux camélias* (65 performances), *Froufrou* (41), and *Adrienne Lecouvreur* (17)—were all dramas named for, and centered on, a tragic female figure; each of them ended with a devastating death scene; none of them had she ever performed in Paris. (She also allowed herself six performances of *Phèdre*, with its own magnificent death scene.) At last the world was seeing "Sarah Bernhardt in . . . " rather than, say, "*Hernani* with Sarah Bernhardt." And it was going to be like that for the next forty years.

Her practice was no longer to adjust her unique talents to the wishes of the writer but to use plays as a conduit for her irrepressible emotional dynamism. *Her* playwrights—Sardou in particular—understood this, and provided her with opportunities to unleash her passion, her fury, her pathos upon the world. Perhaps this was the only way she could assuage the traumas of her childhood and her youth; to safely vent her most powerful feelings. In her alternating suicides and murders she could act out both her often-proclaimed death wish and her rage at her tormentors.

These inevitable death scenes—death by poison, stabbing, garroting, fire, tuberculosis, defenestration—not only gratified her audiences but were undoubtedly essential to her inner life. Her friend, critic, and lover Jules Lemaître put it this way: "She is so habituated to scenes of violence and torture in Sardou that she has little by little lost the facility of expressing ordinary daily sentiments. She becomes herself only when she's killing or when she dies." Meticulously she studied medical symptoms, hospitals, morgues, even executions, to make her death scenes not only effective but accurate. But they all amounted to the same thing: an ecstasy of self-annihilation; extreme emotion projected through the highest levels of craft.

The Bernhardt melodramas didn't depend on her brilliant vocal articulation or her genius for poetry, which is why they proved far more practical than the classics as she maintained her unremitting round of world tours, performing for people who didn't understand her language. How to convey what was taking place? The text became less relevant, and so the longer she played abroad, the faster her delivery grew—few in the audience, even those following the text with translations, could grasp what she was saying. She substituted other means of making her effects: ornate sets and sumptuous costumes, certainly, but more important, a language of exaggerated *plastique* and gesture to replace, or at least supplement, a language of words. And always there was her immense allure. As Lemaître went on to say, "She puts not only her whole heart, soul, and physical grace into her roles but all her sexuality as well." That was always her trump card—the glamour, the excitement, the seductiveness of her personality.

It was this substitution of self for art (as he saw it) that drove George Bernard Shaw to his most incensed invective against her:

> Madame Bernhardt has elected to go around the world
> pretending to kill people with hatchets and hatpins,
> and making, I presume, heaps of money. I wish her
> every success; but I shall certainly not treat her as
> a dramatic artist of the first rank unless she pays me
> well for it.

Above and opposite: Sarah's gestural style in *Phèdre*

The childishly egotistical character of her
acting . . . is not the art of making you think more
highly or feel more deeply, but the art of making
you admire her, pity her, champion her, weep with
her, laugh at her jokes, follow her fortunes breathlessly,
and applaud her wildly when the curtain falls. . . .
And it is always Sarah Bernhardt in her own capacity
who does this to you. The dress, the title of the play,
the order of the words may vary; but the woman is
always the same. She does not enter into the leading
character: she substitutes herself for it.

When Madame Bernhardt gives us pinchbeck
plays and acting that is poor in thought and eked
out with odds and ends stripped from her old parts;
when she rants at us and brings down the house

in a London theatre just as she brings down the house
in a provincial American one, we must tell her that
she can do better than that, and that we will have
nothing less than her best. . . . Of course intoning is
easy—as easy as holding down one key of the accordion
and keeping up a mellifluous smile all the time, but it
dehumanizes speech, and after some minutes becomes
maddening, so that a flash of fun or a burst of rage
is doubly welcome because it for a moment alters that
eternal pitch and timbre.

And in a letter to Ellen Terry, in 1897: "Sara B, though
she has reduced her business to the most mechanical routine
possible, is a worn out hack tragedienne." (Terry, as we have
seen, adored Sarah, both as an actress and as a friend.)

The devastating reviews in which Shaw inveighs against Bernhardt are probably the most famous dramatic criticism we have. But one has to consider them in context. In the mid-1890s, Shaw was at his most polemical in his crusade to popularize Ibsen, and this necessitated a frontal assault on what he saw as outmoded, artificial acting in favor of the naturalism of Duse. Again and again Duse is the stick with which he beats Bernhardt—or at least the Bernhardt of his day. (He seems to have had respect for the old Bernhardt of Racine and Hugo.) In the same way, he uses Ibsen to chastise Rostand—talk about breaking a butterfly on a wheel! He doesn't like Comédie-Française acting, deplores Mounet-Sully and Max, finds the whole French approach to theater hopelessly out of date, synthetic, and irritating. (It doesn't help that he doesn't really know French.)

The importance of Shaw, apart from the sheer joy of reading him, is not the validity (or lack of it) of his judgment, but that he embodies the revolution that was taking place in the theater, a revolution in which Sarah Bernhardt had no place and no interest. She was what she was, and you either fell under her spell or not. He didn't, and it's all to his credit that considerably later in life he confessed in print, "I could never as a dramatic critic be fair to Sarah B., because she was exactly like my Aunt Georgina; but I could not say this at the time, because my Aunt Georgina was alive."

How bad (or good), by our standards, Bernhardt was in the nineties—how we would react to her today, given the chance to flash backward—we can't establish. The range of contemporary response to her acting is almost infinite, from the prudish William Winter, the most important American theater critic of the latter half of the nineteenth century, who acknowledged her talents but abominated the immoral—the vicious—plays she chose to perform (though not as much as he abominated Ibsen), and those like Clement Scott who practically idolized her. Other major English critics admired her unreservedly, while the stern William Archer denounced her in 1895: "Her whole art has become a marvelous, monotonous, and often vulgar virtuosity. She is mannerism incarnate and carried to its highest pitch. Not for ten years or more has she added a single new effect to her arsenal of airs and graces, tremors and tantrums. . . . She is no longer an artist, but an international institution."

Among the wisest words about her art, because they seem both responsive and disinterested (he actually preferred Duse), come from Stark Young, the finest American theater critic of the first half of the twentieth century:

> Bernhardt's genius was essentially public in its character, and there was no wit so slow or so untutored and no eye so dull as not to know that when she played, the universal elements were shaken, and passions that might have been domesticated and blurred became suddenly glamorous and superb. That Bernhardt was limited is obvious. She had a limited range of ideas, such ideas, for instance, as amorous seduction, pain and anger—the famous rage through tears—and the infinite throes of dying. She had certain type conceptions—limited in scope though not in raw force—of the passionate, the ornate, the regal, the comic, the poetic. She had vast monotonies of temperament, however brilliant or strong. Her physical equipment—most of all the immortal voice—was extraordinary but limited in possibilities of style. Bernhardt had, too, an undiluted egotism that very often swamped the play, the other actors, and everything else save the audience's response to herself. To her all art was a passion of self, a splendor of an artist's mood, though to her, also, art was the only important thing in the world.

This is how she was regarded by discriminating critics and audiences who might thrill to her performances but understood what they were thrilling to—Sarah herself. It is certainly not, however, the way she saw herself. In her writings on acting, she insists that the actor must concentrate on his relationship to true feeling, on living the role.

> I contend that it is necessary to feel all the sentiments
> that agitate the soul of the character it is desired
> to represent. The artist's personality must be left
> in his dressing room; his soul must be denuded of his
> own sensations and clothed with the base or noble
> qualities he is called upon to exhibit.

> Do not let us delude ourselves that we can wear the
> vesture of another's soul while preserving our own; do
> not let us imagine for a moment that we can create
> an artificial exterior while maintaining our ordinary
> feelings intact. The actor cannot divide his personality
> between himself and his part; he loses his ego during
> the time he remains on the stage.

> We must make our characters live. And in no way can
> we do this better than by quitting our own personality
> to enter that of another being.

This is some kind of Method acting *avant la lettre*, and diametrically opposed to the way Bernhardt was perceived. Did she really believe that on stage she subordinated herself to the character she was playing? That she subsumed herself in Fédora, Théodora, Tosca, La Dame—even in L'Aiglon and Hamlet? Didn't she grasp that these roles—and all the rest—provided her with objective correlatives for her inner turmoil and release rather than opportunities to understand and convey to the world the inner life of others? And—most improbable of all—did she really not understand the immense power of her own personality?

Certainly others did. Among those who felt it: Mark Twain ("There are five kinds of actresses: bad actresses, fair actresses, good actresses, great actresses—and then there is Sarah Bernhardt"), Freud ("After the first words of her lovely, vibrant voice I felt I had known her for years. . . . A curious being: I can imagine that she needn't be any different in life [from how she is] on the stage"), D. H. Lawrence ("Oh, to see her, and to hear her, a wild creature, a gazelle with a beautiful panther's fascination and fury, sobbing, sighing like a deer sobs, wounded to death, and all the time with the sheen of silk, the glitter of diamonds. . . . She represents the primeval passion of women, and she is fascinating to an extraordinary degree"), Willa Cather ("Her bursts of passion blind one by their vividness. . . . It is like lightning, gone before you see enough of it, and indescribable in its brilliance.")

In a perceptive tribute written just after Sarah's death, Lytton Strachey summed her up:

> Nothing could be further from the truth than to suppose
> that the great Frenchwoman belonged to that futile
> tribe of empty-headed impersonators, who, since Irving,
> have been the particular affliction of the English stage.
> Dazzling divinity though she was, she was also a serious,
> a laborious worker, incessantly occupied—not with
> expensive stage properties, elaborate make-up, and
> historically accurate scenery—but simply with acting.
> Sir Herbert Tree was ineffective because he neither
> knew nor cared how to act; he was content to be a clever
> entertainer. But Sarah Bernhardt's weakness, if weakness
> it can be called, arose from a precisely contrary reason—
> from the very plenitude of so overwhelming a kind
> as to become an obsession.
>
> The result was that this extraordinary genius was
> really to be seen at her most characteristic in plays of
> inferior quality. They gave her what she wanted. She did
> not want—she did not understand—great drama; what
> she did want were opportunities for acting; and this
> was the combination which the *Toscas*, the *Camélias*, and

the rest of them, so happily provided. In them the whole of her enormous virtuosity in the representation of passion had full play; she could contrive thrill after thrill, she could seize and tear the nerves of her audience, she could touch, she could terrify, to the top of her astonishing bent. In them, above all, she could ply her personality to the utmost. All acting must be, to some extent, an exploitation of the personality; but in the acting of Sarah Bernhardt that was the dominating quality—the fundamental element of her art. It was there that her strength, and her weakness, lay. During her best years, her personality remained an artistic instrument; but eventually it became too much for her. It absorbed both herself and her audience; the artist became submerged in the divinity; and what was genuine, courageous, and original in her character was lost sight of in oceans of highly advertised and quite indiscriminate applause.

XXII

The final two decades of Sarah's life—the years following the triumph of *L'Aiglon*—began in her customary way. A procession of new plays, most of them inconsequential, as well as countless revivals of her early triumphs—the Sardou sensations, *Phèdre*, *Adrienne*, *La Dame* (always *La Dame*). The touring went on, often under peculiar circumstances. The English writer Stella Benson, for instance, noted in her 1911 diary,

> Mother and I went up to London. We went to lunch with Aunt Louisa and after that to see Sarah Bernhardt— *Procès de Jeanne d'Arc*—at the Coliseum. She was a long time coming and lots of music hall turns happened before she did. There was a lady in tights who danced and sang, a conjurer who caught live goldfish out of the empty air and did other exciting things, several sets

Sarah as the grief-stricken mother in *Jeanne Doré*

of comedians who knocked each other's hats off and
imitated cocks and hens, a self-satisfied baritone out of
Beecham's opera company, Cecelia Loftus who imper-
sonated celebrities very cleverly and then—Sarah
Bernhardt. She was wonderful but not quite so simple as
I always imagine Joan of Arc to have been at her trial . . .

There were some odd choices of repertory—*Werther*,
Circé (in verse, by an amateur), Racine's *Esther* (she played
King Ahasuerus). There was a succession of short war plays
written especially to accommodate her limited mobility, including an effective patriotic pageant in verse by Eugène Morand
called *Les Cathédrales* (she represented the cathedral of Stras-
bourg); it was one of the pieces she took to the front. There was
the success of Tristan Bernard's *Jeanne Doré* in 1913, a moving
illustration of mother love (she crouches outside her son's

prison cell the night before he's to be executed)—one of the few times she played a woman of the lower classes. There was the triumph of *Athalie*, and worthy efforts to honor her old master Victor Hugo with revivals of two of his prose plays, *Lucrèce Borgia* and *Angelo, tyran de Padoue*. And there were, toward the end, plays by two young men to whom she was connected by sentiment and history (and who despised each other, each viciously disparaging the other's work), Maurice Rostand and Louis Verneuil. It was in the latter's *Daniel* (1920) that, barely leaving her bed, she impersonated the dying thirty-year-old drug addict. Rouben Mamoulian, the famous stage and film director-to-be, wrote of this performance more than thirty-five years afterward:

> Propped with pillows, in bed, she was dying. In the last few seconds, while the stream of life was still flowing through her heart, she sat up straight. Suddenly something strange and powerful crept into her voice and into the face, in spite of the blank, doll-like mask of enamel that covered it. A few more half-whispered words and life was no more.
>
> Now, I'm sure any other actress dying in this particular scene would have fallen back onto the pillows, her arms gracefully at her sides, her face pale against the frame of curly hair, lying on the pillows for the whole audience to see, with its last smile of radiance, serenity, sadness or what have you. Not so with Bernhardt. Unexpectedly, with a shock that made you sit up and quiver in your chair, she fell forward, like a figure of lead, heavy and limp, her arms collapsing pathetically and awkwardly at her side, palms up. She moved no more. There was death—stark, final, unpremeditated. Seemingly so, of course—but that was high art. That was the one touch that proclaimed: Sarah Bernhardt the great is on that stage! The house rocked with an immediate fury of applause. People were jumping up and down on their

Sarah as the young dope addict in *Daniel*

seats. There were many curtain calls. Her bows were
beautifully prearranged. She stood in the middle of the
stage, her arms outstretched horizontally supported
by two actors, her head bowed low—a complete image
of Christ on the Cross. She did not change the position
through all the curtain calls, except occasionally to

lift her head and then to droop it again on her chest.
I have never heard so much noise in the theater. I joined
in the general tumult by applauding until my hands
hurt, and yelling lustily at the top of my voice.

There's a film of this death scene. Bernhardt is white-faced, restrained, compelling, bizarre.

Her film career was lucrative, but the films themselves do not for the most part help her reputation—she was interested in the new medium but soon realized that she would never master it. Her broadly gestural acting—the arms thrown wide open, the hands clutching at the head—looks overwrought and old-fashioned on the screen, and her belief that she still looked young was fatally undermined when she saw herself. (It's said that she fainted when she saw the film of *La Dame aux camélias*, and she actually suppressed her *La Tosca*.)

The movie of hers that had the widest circulation—that made her the first international movie star (at the age of sixty-eight)—was her *Queen Elizabeth* or *Elizabeth, Queen of England*, filmed in 1912. Adolph Zukor, who would go on to reign over Paramount until he was eighty-six, had formed a company called Famous Players, and he put up forty thousand dollars to help get *Elizabeth* made and to acquire the American rights. Sarah had appeared recently (and not successfully) in an Elizabeth play, but a four-reel movie of the most famous actress in the world was a major cultural event—the most prestigious film yet presented to the public. Zukor made the most of it, charging exhibitors record-high prices and releasing it under his company's banner—"Famous Players in Famous Plays"—to extraordinary acclaim. Not only was it the first successful feature film, but it attracted educated people—upper-class people—to the movies for the first time. As Zukor remarks in his memoirs, "Her performance was of historical importance because it went a long way toward breaking down the prejudice of theatrical people toward the screen."

Yet in that same year of 1912, the respected American critic Percy Hammond could write of her:

> It is said that the most interesting period in an artiste's career is that of her decadence. If that be true, Madame Sarah has reached a perihelion. For years she has been the more or less glittering shell of an actress, the illustration of a marvelous system, the memory of a wonderful personality, a virtuoso of tradition, the Tom Thumb, the White Elephant, the Sarah Barnum of the theater. Skilful, plucky, gallant, enduring, energetic, and alas! senile, she has come before us in farewell tour after farewell tour, a phenomenon, fascinating, amazing in some respects, but always an exhibition.
>
> To me in every role she is the Mona Lisa, disinterested, semi-smiling, and inscrutable save for the knowledge that she insists on being paid every night in fresh $100 dollar bills. Her effective moments in "Lucrece Borgia" last evening recurred like a habit, automatic. Sheer technique is this habit, a matter

of eyes and mouth and hands. The echo of a great
imagination and, perhaps, a great emotion is there,
but it is old and empty and shrunken, and like
something in a tomb. When she exhales her lines,
the exhalation is musty. It is too late, and it is too bad.

It was increasingly evident, then, that her work was
eroding and that her kind of declamatory acting was a thing
of the past. Crowds of people still came to see her, but more
and more as one goes to see a famous monument. Parents
would bring their children so that they could one day tell
their children (and grandchildren) that they had seen the great
Sarah Bernhardt act. Her fame was certainly undiminished—
indeed, she was possibly more famous than ever—but less
as an actress than as a worshiped relic of another era. Her
patriotism, her largeness of spirit, her refusal to acknowledge
age or limitation had combined to turn her into a national
treasure, a cultural landmark, a great woman of France—a
symbol of France—if no longer a creative force. Forgotten were
the scandals, the waywardness, the provocations. Even her
Jewishness was forgotten.

Many of her closest friends were gone—Rostand (in the
great postwar flu epidemic), Clairin, Geoffroy, Pozzi (assassinated by a madman). Her older granddaughter, Simone, had
married an English businessman and lived in London. Maurice
was still with her, but he himself was unwell, suffering from
Parkinson's disease. He had gone on co-directing Sarah's theater, occasionally writing or co-writing an insubstantial play,
and living his life of a pampered and distinguished aging play-
boy. Louis Verneuil first met him in 1919, when he was nearly
fifty-five, "tall, slim, with fine features," and undoubtedly one
of the handsomest men of his generation. "But *paralysis agitans*,
which had attacked him in 1914 and had since been gradually
increasing, had aged him prematurely. At first only the little
finger of his right hand was affected. Soon this constant tremor

spread to all his fingers, then to his hand, and now to his fore-arm. Henceforth, night and day, he did not know what it was to be still. As early as 1919 he had to hold his right hand with his left in order to write." Maurice would die in 1928, only five years after his mother. (At least she was spared his death.)

Her own health had been steadily deteriorating for many years—the disaster of her leg and the shock of the amputation, the years battling uremic disorders—so that having seemed preternaturally young for so long, she now appeared prematurely aged.

Maurice and Lysiane tried to persuade her to retire from the stage, to rest in the country, but she answered them less than tactfully: "Then who will pay your debts, Maurice? Who will put on your Verneuil's plays, Lysiane?" The show went on. Her final performance before an audience—the play was Verneuil's *Régine Armand*—took place on November 29, 1922, in Turin. Appropriately, she was on the road, and in the very city where she had inspired Duse forty years earlier. (Duse would outlive her by less than a year.)

Among her visitors in her final months was Colette, who immediately recorded her impressions:

> I had received an invitation which was more like a com-mand. "Madame Bernhardt expects you for lunch on such and such a day." I had never seen her so close. There she was at the end of a long gallery, the *raison d'être* of a somewhat funereal museum, filled with potted palms, sprays of dried flowers, commemorative plaques, and tributes. Her amputation no longer mattered, enveloped as she was in fold after fold of some dark material. Her white face and small hands still glowed like bruised flowers. I never wearied of looking at her blue eyes, which seemed to change color with each lively movement of her small imperious head.
>
> Sarah disappeared just before lunch, whisked away by stage machinery, or simply by faithful arms. We found

Sarah in her mid-seventies

her on the floor above, seated at table in her gothic throne. She ate, or seemed to eat. She became animated each time the conversation turned to the theater. Her critical sense, her opinions, and her way of expressing herself were extraordinary. She was mischievously severe about an actress who had just attempted to play *L'Aiglon*. "The poor dear isn't man enough to make us forget she's a woman, and not woman enough to be appealing."

She stopped talking theater only long enough to attend to a large earthenware coffeepot which was brought to the table. She measured out the ground coffee, wet it with boiling water, filled our cups, and waited for our well-earned praise. "Don't I make coffee every bit as well as Catulle Mendès?" she asked as she leaned toward me from the height of her majestic chair.

I record here one of the last gestures of the tragedienne approaching her eightieth year: a delicate faded hand offering a full cup; the cornflower blue of her eyes, so young, caught in a web of wrinkles; the laughing interrogative coquetry of the turn of the head. And that indomitable, endless desire to charm, to charm again, to charm even unto the gates of death.

Not that she acknowledged that her career was over, let alone that she was approaching her death. A few months before she died, she was interviewed by Alexander Woollcott and told him that she was contemplating another American tour. But this time not such a long one, since she was "much too old for such cross-country junketing. . . . Of course, I shall play Boston and New York and Philadelphia and Washington. And perhaps Buffalo and Cleveland and Detroit and Kansas City and St. Louis and Denver and San Francisco . . . " Of course. How could she stop? Like Pavlova, like Nureyev—like Duse—she was a driven performer, a *monstre sacré*, endlessly working at her art, eternally touring.

And then came a stroke of luck: Sacha Guitry, by now the golden boy of French theater, had written a delicious part for her in a new play, a modern play, called *Un Sujet de roman* (A subject for a novel). It would be a family affair, also featuring Sacha himself, his wife—the wonderful singer-actress Yvonne Printemps—and his father, Lucien, Sarah's old partner and dear friend.

Rehearsals went well, with every due attention being paid to Sarah, given her frailty. In his memoirs, Sacha recalls the dress rehearsal:

Sarah had a long speech in the last act. It was the terrible scene in which the woman confesses that she understands her husband and when he, who despises her, finds it in himself to forgive her. Sarah was at the peak of her powers that day. With no lapse of memory she spoke in a terrifyingly thin, disjointed, magnificent, heart-rending voice. My father was seated at a table opposite her, his hat pulled down over his eyes. When she finished, instead of answering, he reached for her hand and muttered: "Wait a moment." He could not go on. He was weeping. Theater? But the theater was their life, their death, their everything. When we finished, Sarah asked if she could rest in my dressing room. But toward 7 o'clock she began to choke and we took her home.

Alas, she never recovered—never again set foot in a theater. The play went on without her, another actress playing her role, and in her bed on opening night she mouthed her lines when she knew the curtain had gone up.

Even so, unable to leave her house, she wasn't finished: an offer for a film called *La Voyante* (The Fortune Teller). The writer was her Sacha, her co-stars included Lili Damita and the great Harry Baur. Tactfully it was arranged that they film in her house, and she was brought downstairs on the days her scenes were being shot. But she was unable to finish; the uremia that she had survived in 1917 finally defeated her.

For two months she lingered, with Maurice and his family, Louise Abbéma, and her doctor tending her. A few intimates—Reynaldo Hahn, Maurice Rostand—were allowed to visit. As she steadily slipped away, she received last rites. For several days crowds gathered outside her house and reporters stood by, waiting for her death. "I'll keep them dangling," she said with a smile. "They've tortured me all my life, now I'll torture them." These were her last words, as she died in Maurice's arms. At eight in the evening on March 26, 1923, her doctor leaned from a window and announced to the crowd waiting below, "Madame Sarah Bernhardt is dead." When the news reached her theater, during the first act of a performance

Sarah's funeral cortège approaching her theater

of *L'Aiglon*, the curtain was lowered, the audience silently filed out, and the actors, still in costume and makeup, left for her house to bid her farewell.

For three days many thousands of people filed past her body, laid out in her famous coffin, the ribbon of the Légion d'Honneur on her breast. Her funeral was given by the municipal council of Paris. Hundreds of thousands of people—some say half a million—lined the streets, some kneeling, many weeping, as the coffin was carried first to the Church of St. François de Sales, then—pausing for a few moments outside the Théâtre Sarah Bernhardt—on to the Père-Lachaise cemetery. Paris had seen nothing like it since the funeral of Victor Hugo almost forty years before.

Years earlier she had pronounced a kind of epitaph for herself: "The good God has permitted me a triumphant life. I believe it will be triumphant to the end." On her tombstone, however, it merely said SARAH BERNHARDT—her dates were added later—and that was enough. All of France, all the world, knew who she was.

❈ Epilogue ❧

IN 1950, MORE than a quarter of a century after Sarah's death,
her beloved Maurice Rostand—of whom it was said that he
adored her so much that he had his hair curled and dyed to
resemble hers, and even made up his face to look like hers—
wrote in his memoirs, "Ah! For beings like Sarah, death is
not only an end, it's a beginning as well. The life may be
sundered, but the legend goes on. Sarah has not been forgotten, nor has she been replaced. . . . Her mysterious throne remains empty!"

Today, well into the next millennium, we see how accurate his prophecy has been. To an extraordinary degree, the
name and reputation of this nineteenth-century actress have
retained their potency. To begin with, of course, her death unleashed a tidal wave of commentary. The *Times* of London obit-
uary can stand for all the others:

> No temperament more histrionic than Mme Bernhardt's
> has, perhaps, ever existed. To read her memoirs is
> to live in a whirl of passions and adventures—floods
> of tears, tornadoes of rage, deathly sickness and
> incomparable health and energy, deeds of reckless

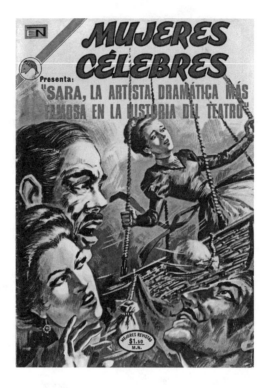

bravado, caprices indescribable and enormous. The
marvelous voice of gold, that wide range of beautiful
movement, queenly, sinuous, terrible, alluring, that
intensity of passion and that bewitching sweetness
have brought men and women of all degrees—from
professional critics to ranchers, from anarchists
to kings, from men of pleasure to Puritan ladies—in
homage to her feet.

A flood of memoirs and biographies was to follow. And
the literature continues to grow: In recent years alone there
have been well over a dozen books, some highly specialized, some general, at least three novels, and—particularly charming—one of the "Lucky Luke" graphic novels that
have been almost as popular with kids in France as *Tintin* and

Astérix. (Sarah is on the Wild West leg of her first American tour, and President Rutherford B. Hayes entrusts her safety to Cowboy Luke.) There have been a movie, *The Incredible Sarah*, with an insanely miscast Glenda Jackson; a listless French documentary with voice-over by Susan Sontag; and, two or three years ago, an overwrought modern dance work by Jacqulyn Buglisi.

In the 1940s and 1950s Sarah was a handy reference point for Hollywood, from Marilyn Monroe in *The Seven Year Itch* ("Every time I show my teeth on television, I'm appearing before more people than Sarah Bernhardt appeared before in her whole career"), to Judy Garland as a highly unlikely L'Aiglon in *Babes on Broadway*, to an embarrassingly inappropriate Ginger Rogers as a very young Sarah intoning "La

The spiral …
and caricatured by Léandre

Marseillaise" in *The Barkleys of Broadway*. The audiences for these movies understood exactly who she had been and what she stood for. According to *Sarah Bernhardt: The Art of High Drama*, the superb companion book to the revelatory 2005 Bernhardt exhibition at New York's Jewish Museum, among the other actors who evoke her name in films are John Barrymore in *Twentieth Century*, Joseph Cotten in *Portrait of Jennie*, Jane Powell in *Nancy Goes to Rio*, Julie Andrews in *Star!* and Nicole Kidman in *Moulin Rouge*. And Hollywood has acknowledged her officially: She has a star in the Hollywood Walk of Fame at 1751 Vine Street. (So does Johnny Carson; Joan Crawford is at 1750.) France, too, has canonized her: In 1945 she appeared on a postage stamp, the first woman to do so other than Madame Curie—who had to share the honor with her husband.

As for merchandise, eBay can supply you with the 1986 "Dame aux Camélias" memorial plate, the book of Sarah Bernhardt paper dolls, the Madame Alexander Sarah Bernhardt doll, the "assymetrical" [*sic*] Sarah Bernhardt earrings, and the "Heirloom" Sarah Bernhardt peony, as well as countless re-productions of the famous art nouveau posters by Mucha and a variety of embroidery patterns based on them—stitch your own Gismonda! (Probably no longer available: copies of the 1973 Mexican comic book called *Sara, la Artista Dramática Más Famosa en la Historia del Teatro*.) You probably can, however, still acquire copies of Andy Warhol's silkscreen portrait of Sarah, done for his series Ten Portraits of Jews of the Twentieth Century, as well as a Currier and Ives print of her, with flaming red hair, from her first American tour—a lunatic juxtaposition of artists if ever there was one.

Her influence on the plastic arts and on couture was im-measurable. The way she stood and sat, the clothes she wore, embodied the art nouveau aesthetic. "It's noteworthy," Reynaldo Hahn wrote,

> that for all her "dresses of ceremony," for whatever
> occasion they are intended, she insists on that same Sarah
> Bernhardt-esque cut—a bodice draped to her figure and
> a skirt that clings more tightly around the legs than
> around the hips, giving the appearance of encircling her
> in a spiral. Moreover, a spiral has always been the formula
> for Sarah. In all her movements the principle of the
> spiral obtains. When she sits, note that she sits in a spiral,
> her dress swirling round her, her train on the ground
> completing the spiral design which her head and bust
> carry out in the opposite direction above.

Once she had entered her Sardou phase, most of what she wore and decorated herself with—unless she was in Phèdre's classic

Three of Sarah's most famous headpieces: *Théodora*, King Ahasuerus in *Esther*, and ...

white robes or in snug male garb—was overwhelmingly ornate: She was brocaded and encrusted with jewels; be-frilled and be-furred; cameoed and caped; diademed and crowned. And all these items were magnificently designed and crafted—high art nouveau artisanship by such designers as Lalique and Mucha himself, whose famous snake bracelet was created for *Cléopâtre*. She was a walking museum.

Finally, Sarah has been credited with being the model for characters in novels by two of the world's greatest novelists. Is she really, as is frequently maintained, Miriam Rooth in Henry James's *The Tragic Muse* of 1890? James doesn't mention her in his extended introduction to the novel written for the New York Edition of his work, and her personal story is nothing like Miriam's, but they share a heightened voracity for their art, and for life. And—with more than thirty years of her career still in

La Princesse lointaine

the future—James uncannily predicted what her life was to be, racketing around the world "with populations and deputations, reporters and photographers, placards and interviews and banquets, steamers, railroads, dollars, diamonds, speeches and artistic ruin all jumbled into her train." Yet, prescient as always, he also foretold that "putting strange accidents aside, Miriam would go further than any one had gone, in England at least and within the memory of man." (Oddly, the portrait on the cover of the Penguin Classics edition of *The Tragic Muse* is of Rachel, not Sarah.)

But no one can doubt that Sarah is Proust's chief source for the figure of the great actress Berma in *In Search of Lost Time*—not in terms of plot, but in the way she represents a crucial development in his thinking about the artistic imagination. Berma is threaded throughout the novel, both as an active character and as a referent—along with Elstir the painter and Vinteuil the composer—for the author's eternal quest to grasp the nature of art and the artist.

In the mind of Marcel, Proust's narrator, Berma is inescapably identified with her performances as Phèdre. Here, from *The Guermantes Way*, is a ravishing (and exhausting) passage that suggests the power and complexity of his idea of Bernhardt-as-Berma-as-artist:

> Berma's arms, which the lines of verse themselves by
> the same emissive force that made the voice issue
> from her lips, seemed to raise on to her bosom like leaves
> displaced by a gush of water; her stage presence, her
> poses, which she had gradually built up, which she was
> to modify yet further, and which were based upon
> reasonings altogether more profound than those of
> which traces could be seen in the gestures of her fellow-
> actors, but reasonings that had lost their original
> deliberation, had melted into a sort of radiance whereby
> they sent throbbing, round the person of the heroine,
> rich and complex elements which the fascinated
> spectator nevertheless took not for a triumph of dramatic
> artistry but for a manifestation of life; those white
> veils themselves, which, tenuous and clinging, seemed
> to be of a living substance and to have been woven
> by the suffering, half-pagan, half-Jansenist, around
> which they drew themselves like a frail and shrinking
> cocoon—all these, voice, posture, gestures, veils,
> round this embodiment of an idea which a line of poetry
> is (an embodiment that, unlike our human bodies,
> is not an opaque screen, but a purified, spiritualized
> garment), were merely additional envelopes which,
> instead of concealing, showed up in greater splendor
> the soul that had assimilated them to itself and had
> spread itself through them, lava-flows of different
> substances, grown translucent, the superimposition
> of which causes only a richer refraction of the imprisoned

central ray that pierces through them, and makes
more extensive, more precious and more beautiful the
flame-drenched matter in which it is enshrined.
So Berma's interpretation was, around Racine's work, a
second work, quickened also by the breath of genius.

And so Sarah Bernhardt is still with us—in Proust and
Ginger Rogers, art nouveau and peonies and paper dolls. Her
name remains the paradigm for "Great Actress," the way the
name of Pavlova does for "Ballerina" or Einstein for "Genius."
She is still the most famous of all Frenchwomen after Joan
of Arc and the most famous French personality of the nineteenth century after Napoléon. But perhaps the most lingering
effect of her name and fame resides in the minds of the untold
number of women (so many of them Jewish—I know a dozen
of them) who, when they were acting up as little girls, were
lovingly scolded by their parents with the words, "You're a regular Sarah Bernhardt!"*

*I wonder whether one of them was Barbra Streisand, who in a 2009 interview
in the *Los Angeles Times*, said, "When we were making the film *Hello, Dolly!* in
1968, they asked me what kind of furnishing did I want in the trailer. I said I
wanted Sarah Bernhardt's railway car. And, boy, that's what I got."

A NOTE ON SOURCES

The Bernhardt literature is vast, in both French and English. Unfortunately, it's also extremely contradictory. The absence of documentation, plus Bernhardt's own impulses toward self-dramatization and away from strict veracity, leaves biographers at the mercy of their *own* impulses: Do I choose to believe X's account? Y's? Z's?

There are three substantial biographies in English, all long out of print. Cornelia Otis Skinner's best-selling *Madame Sarah* has the advantage of being written by an actress, sympathetic to the most famous of actresses and understanding of her dilemmas and choices. Although Skinner is not a scholar, she worked diligently, and her book is both entertaining and responsible, if not entirely reliable.

Ruth Brandon's *Being Divine* goes deepest into Bernhardt's psychology, and offers many acute perceptions. It has a measured feminist approach and tells the story feelingly. Although Brandon does an excellent job with the professional life, her great strengths come into play with the personal. You feel she understands Sarah, so that you do too.

Arthur Gold and Robert Fizdale's *The Divine Sarah* (I was involved with its publication) reflect their brilliant grasp of the social and artistic climate of Sarah's Paris. Their previous book, *Misia*, about Diaghilev's great friend and sponsor Misia Sert, was a perfect preparation for Sarah, and further assured their entrée into what was left of Sarah's world. (Their passion for gossip was an essential element of both their books. We owe to them, for instance, the recovery and translation of the letters between Sarah and Mounet-Sully.) They are also immensely readable.

Joanna Richardson's biography, *Sarah Bernhardt*, is more compressed than those referred to above, but it's a very satisfactory walk through the material; her *Sarah Bernhardt and Her World* is mostly pictorial, helping to reveal Sarah's person and immediate surround as well as the context she moved in.

There are, of course, a number of full-scale lives in French. In 2006, one by Henri Gidel, a decent but not very original reworking of old ground; in 2009, one by Hélène Tierchant, with a considerable amount of new and riveting anecdote, though light on documentation. Philippe Jullian (1977) is fascinating because indiscreet. André Castelot (1973) is as always informed and engaging, but he's hardly definitive.

The most important Bernhardt book in French was written, during World War II and published posthumously in Geneva, by a Swiss, Ernest Pronier. It's titled *Une Vie au théâtre*, and it is indeed an anatomy of Sarah's life in the theater, as well as a sensitive and sympathetic account of her life and exploration of her surround (it begins with a highly useful account of the major actresses who preceded her and were her contemporaries). But its great achievement is its painstaking, almost obsessive account of what roles she played, where she played them, and frequently *how* she played them. The generous and modest Pronier, with his extraordinary detective work, established the record of Bernhardt's career on which all her biographers since 1941 have depended.

Naturally, Bernhardt's own memoirs are central to our knowledge of her life up to and through her first American tour of 1880–1881. Not that they're reliable, but for the most part, they're what we have—and they're intensely readable. Both her granddaughter Lysiane and Lysiane's husband, Louis Verneuil, wrote biographies based on discussions held with her in the year or two before she died. A biography by Jules Huret, published in 1898, was the result of extended interviews she gave him with a book in mind.

Books by two women who knew Sarah well—Marie Colombier and Thérèse Berton—are filled with animus, yet provide us with essential data and illuminations that, alas, have to be taken with tablespoons of salt.

There are numerous memoirs by friends and associates who loved her, none more perceptive and appreciative than that by the wonderful composer Reynaldo Hahn.

The most detailed and perceptive books anatomizing her acting are both by the American scholar Gerda Taranow: *Sarah Bernhardt: The Art within the Legend* and *The Bernhardt Hamlet: Culture and Context*. There are scholarly books devoted to her first American tour, to her Australian tour, to her touring in Canada. There are the collected reviews of major French critics, most important of whom is Francisque Sarcey. (Luckily for me, I had acquired the seven volumes of them on a whim almost fifty years before beginning work on this book—and had never looked at them until now.)

There are the collected reviews of many English and American theater critics, including Henry James's *The Scenic Art* and of course the three volumes of George Bernard Shaw's *Theater in the Nineties* and Max Beerbohm's *Around Theatres*. Lytton Strachey and Maurice Baring are among the most persuasive commentators about her person and her art. David Menefee's *Sarah Bernhardt in the Theatre of Films and Sound Recordings* is essential to tracking her career in these areas.

Of the many books focused on her iconography, the most extensive and impressive in English is *Sarah Bernhardt: The Art of High Drama*, the companion volume to the superb Bernhardt exhibition at New York's Jewish Museum, edited by Carol Ockman and Kenneth E. Silver; it also includes a series of highly informative essays.

There are the many novels about her, including several recent ones, all of them exploitative and none of them convincing.

And then there's everything else—including what must be the most unlikely book ever written about her: Françoise Sagan's *Dear Sarah Bernhardt*, an epistolary exchange between Sagan and the long-dead Sarah. It's hardly reliable, but it's a fascination!

BIBLIOGRAPHY

Arthur, George. *Sarah Bernhardt*. London: Heinemann, 1923.

Aston, Elaine. *Sarah Bernhardt: A French Actress on the English Stage*. Oxford: Berg, 1989.

Baring, Maurice. *Maurice Baring Restored: Selections from His Work*. Ed. Paul Horgan. New York: Farrar, Straus and Giroux, 1970.

————. *The Puppet Show of Memory*. Boston: Little, Brown, 1922.

————. *Sarah Bernhardt*. New York: D. Appleton-Century, 1934.

Beerbohm, Max. *Around Theatres*. New York: Knopf, 1930.

Bernhardt, Lysiane. *Sarah Bernhardt, My Grandmother*. London: Hurst and Blackett, 1949.

Bernhardt, Sarah. *Memories of My Life: Being My Personal, Professional, and Social Recollections as Woman and Artist*. New York: Appleton, 1907.

————. *The Art of the Theatre*. Trans. H. J. Stenning. London: Geoffrey Bles, 1924.

Bolitho, William. *Leviathan*. New York: Harper and Brothers, 1924.

Brandon, Ruth. *Being Divine: A Biography of Sarah Berhardt*. London: Secker and Warburg, 1991.

Brownstein, Rachel M. *Tragic Muse: Rachel of the Comédie-Française*. New York: Knopf, 1993.

Campbell, Mrs. Patrick [Beatrice Stella Cornwallis-West]. *My Life and Some Letters*. New York: Dodd, Mead, 1922.

Castelot, André. *Sarah Bernhardt*. Paris: Le Livre Contemporain, 1961.

Cocteau, Jean. *Souvenir Portraits: Paris in the Belle Epoque*. Paris: Grasset, 1935.

Colombier, Marie. *The Life and Memoirs of Sarah Barnum*. New York: Munro, 1884.

————. *Le Voyage de Sarah Bernhardt en Amérique*. Paris: Maurice Dreyfous, 1882.

Dickens, Charles. *The Letters of Charles Dickens*. Vol. 8, *1856–1858*, ed. Graham Story and Kathleen Tillotson. Oxford: Clarendon, 1995.

Dupont-Nivel, Jean. *Sarah Bernhardt: Reine de théâtre et souveraine de Belle-Île-en-Mer*. Rennes: Ouest-France, 1996.

Dussane, Béatrix. *Dieux des planches*. Paris: Flammarion, 1964.

Emboden, William. *Sarah Bernhardt*. London: Studio Vista, 1974.

Farrar, Geraldine. *Such Sweet Compulsion: The Autobiography of Geraldine Farrar*. New York: Greystone, 1938.

Feuillet, Mme. Octave [Valérie Marie Elvire Dubois Feuillet]. *Souvenirs et Correspondances*. Paris: Calmann Lévy, 1896.

Fraser, Corille. *Come to Dazzle: Sarah Bernhardt's Australian Tour*. Sydney: Currency, 1998.

Geller, G. G. *Sarah Bernhardt, Divine Eccentric*. New York: Frederick A. Stokes, 1933.

Gidel, Henri. *Sarah Bernhardt: Biographie.* Paris: Flammarion, 2006.

Gold, Arthur, and Robert Fizdale. *The Divine Sarah: A Life of Sarah Bernhardt.* New York: Knopf, 1991.

Goncourt, Edmond de. *La Faustin.* Trans. G. F. Monkshood and I. R. N. K. St. Tristan. London: Lotus, 1906.

Goncourt, Edmond de, and Jules de Goncourt. *Journals: Mémoires de la vie littéraire.* Paris: G. Charpentier, 1887–1888.

Guibert, Noëlle. *Portrait(s) de Sarah Bernhardt.* Paris: Bibliothèque nationale de France, 2000.

Guilbert, Yvette. *La Chanson de ma vie (mes mémoires).* Paris: B. Grasset, 1927.

Guitry, Sacha. *Si j'ai bonne mémoire.* Paris, 1934.

Hahn, Reynaldo. *Sarah Bernhardt: Impressions.* Trans. Ethel Thompson. London: Elkin Mathews, 1932.

Hammond, Percy. *This Atom in the Audience: A Digest of Reviews and Comment.* New York: Ferris, 1940.

Hatch, Alden. *Red Carpet for Mamie.* New York: Holt, 1954.

Hathorn, Ramon. *Our Lady of the Snows: Sarah Bernhardt in Canada.* New York: Lang, 1996.

Huret, Jules. *Sarah Bernhardt.* Trans. G. A. Raper. London: Chapman and Hall, 1899.

James, Henry. *The Scenic Art: Notes on Acting and the Drama, 1872–1901.* Ed. Allan Wade. New Brunswick, N.J.: Rutgers University Press, 1948.

———. *The Tragic Muse.* Boston: Houghton Mifflin, 1890.

Jullian, Philippe. *Sarah Bernhardt.* Paris: Balland, 1977.

Kirsch, Adam. *Benjamin Disraeli.* New York: Nextbook/Schocken, 2008.

Knapp, Bettina Liebowitz, and Myra Chipman. *That Was Yvette: The Biography of Yvette Guilbert, the Great Diseuse.* New York: Holt, Rinehart and Winston, 1964.

Lifar, Serge. *The Three Graces: Anna Pavlova, Tamara Karsavina, Olga Spessivtzeva: The Legends and the Truth.* Trans. Gerard Hopkins. London: Cassell, 1959.

Lorcey, Jacques. *Sarah Bernhardt: L'Art et la vie.* Paris: Séguier, 2005.

MacCarthy, Desmond. *Drama.* London: Putnam, 1940.

Mamoulian, Rouben. "Bernhardt versus Duse." *Theatre Arts,* September 1957.

Marks, Patricia. *Sarah Bernhardt's First American Theatrical Tour, 1880–1881.* Jefferson, N.C.: McFarland, 2003.

Melba, Nellie. *Melodies and Memories.* London: T. Butterworth, 1925.

Menefee, David. *Sarah Bernhardt in the Theatre of Films and Sound Recordings.* Jefferson, N.C.: McFarland, 2003.

Moreno, Marguerite. *Souvenirs de ma vie.* Paris: Flore, 1948.

Morris, Xavier Fauche, and Jean Léturgie. *Lucky Luke: Sarah Bernhardt.* Paris: Dargaud, 1982.

Ockman, Carol, and Kenneth E. Silver. *Sarah Bernhardt: The Art of High Drama.* New York: Jewish Museum; New Haven: Yale University Press, 2005.

Pougy, Liane de. *My Blue Notebooks.* New York: Harper and Row, 1979.

Pronier, Ernest. *Une Vie au théâtre: Sarah Bernhardt.* Geneva: Jullien, 1942.

Proust, Marcel. *The Guermantes Way.* Trans. C. K. Scott Moncrieff. London: Chatto and Windus, 1925.

Renard, Jules. *Journal*. Paris: Gallimard, 1935.

Richardson, Joanna. *Sarah Bernhardt*. London: Reinhardt, 1959.

———. *Sarah Bernhardt and Her World*. New York: Putnam, 1977.

Robertson, W. Graham. *Life Was Worth Living: The Reminiscences of W. Graham Robertson*. New York: Harper, 1931.

Rostand, Maurice. *Sarah Bernhardt*. Paris: Calmann-Levy, 1950.

Rueff, Suze. *I Knew Sarah Bernhardt*. London: Muller, 1951.

Sagan, Françoise. *Dear Sarah Bernhardt*. Trans. Sabine Destrée. New York: Seaver, 1988.

Sarcey, Francisque. *Quarante Ans de Théâtre*. Paris: Bibliothèque des Annales politiques et littéraires, 1900–1902.

Scott, Clement. *Some Notable "Hamlets" of the Present Time (Sarah Bernhardt, Henry Irving, Wilson Barrett, Beerbohm Tree, and Forbes Robertson)*. London: Greening, 1905.

Shaw, George Bernard. *Our Theatres in the Nineties*. New York: Brentano's, 1906.

Skinner, Cornelia Otis. *Madame Sarah*. Boston: Houghton Mifflin, 1967.

Spivakoff, Pierre. *Sarah Bernhardt vue par les Nadar*. Paris: Herscher, 1982.

Strachey, Lytton. "Sarah Bernhardt." *The Nation and the Athenaeum*, May 5, 1923. Collected in *Biographical Essays*. New York: Harcourt, Brace, 1949.

Taranow, Gerda. *The Bernhardt Hamlet: Culture and Context*. New York: Lang, 1996.

———. *Sarah Bernhardt: The Art within the Legend*. Princeton: Princeton University Press, 1972.

Tellegen, Lou. *Women Have Been Kind*. New York: Vanguard, 1931.

Terry, Ellen. *The Story of My Life: Recollections and Reflections*. New York: McClure, 1908.

Tierchant, Hélène. *Sarah Bernhardt: Madame "Quand même."* Paris: Editions SW Télémaque, 2009.

Winter, William. *Shadows of the Stage*. Vol. 2. New York: Macmillan, 1893.

Verneuil, Louis. *The Fabulous Life of Sarah Bernhardt*. Trans. Ernest Boyd. New York: Harper and Brothers, 1942.

Vizetelly, Ernest Alfred. *Paris and Her People under the Third Republic*. London: Chatto and Windus, 1919.

Webster, Margaret. *The Same Only Different: Five Generations of a Great Theatre Family*. New York: Knopf, 1969.

Woon, Basil, from material supplied by Mme. Pierre Berton. *The Real Sarah Bernhardt, Whom Her Audiences Never Knew*. New York: Boni and Liveright, 1924.

Young, Stark. *The Flower in Drama* and *Glamour: Theatre Essays and Criticism*. New York: Scribner's, 1955.

Zukor, Adolph, with Dale Kramer. *The Public Is Never Wrong: The Autobiography of Adolph Zukor*. Putnam, 1953.

ACKNOWLEDGMENTS

I would like to thank the following people for advice, aid, and comfort along the way.

Mindy Aloff, Adam Begley, Anka Begley, Mary Blume, the late Marie-Claude de Brunhoff, Carolyn Burke, Robert Cornfield, the late Barbara Epstein, Mimi Gnoli (for the author photograph), Anabel Goff-Davis, Yasmine Ergas, Lizzie Gottlieb, Richard Howard, Andy Hughes (for helping so generously with the art), Diane Johnson, Julie Kavanaugh, Alastair Macaulay, Janet Malcolm, Daniel Mendelsohn, Agnès Montenay, Richard Overstreet (for the photograph of Sarah's tombstone), Claudia Roth Pierpont, Sarah Rothbard (for everything), Robert Silvers, Maria Tucci, and the staff of the Theater Collection at the New York Public Library of Performing Arts at Lincoln Center.

And at Yale University Press: Ileene Smith, my editor, first for insisting I write this book, then for so cheerfully and convincingly explaining my trade-publishing ways to this university press—and vice versa; Dan Heaton, my text editor, for his scrupulous work and broad knowledge, and for making the whole process so easy and so much fun; Nancy Ovedovitz, head of the design department, for allowing me to participate (interfere?) so vigorously in the book's design; Chris Coffin, the head of production, for understanding—and so patiently and good-humoredly responding to—my concerns; Donna Anstey, whose sensible, practical, and flexible understanding of permissions exactly matches mine; and to the sympathetic, indefatigable, and talented Gregg Chase, for working with me so closely and happily on the actual design.

INDEX

JEWISH LIVES is a major series of brief, interpretive biography designed to illuminate the imprint of eminent Jewish figures upon literature, religion, philosophy, politics, cultural and economic life, and the arts and sciences. Subjects are paired with authors to elicit lively, deeply informed books that explore the breadth and complexity of Jewish experience from antiquity through the present.

Jewish Lives is a partnership of Yale University Press and the Leon D. Black Foundation.

Anita Shapira and Steven J. Zipperstein are series editors.